Lawyers Practice and Procedure Series

Practice and Procedure in Magistrates' Courts

by C H Moiser
Solicitor, Justices' Clerk for Plymouth

Second edition

London
Fourmat Publishing
1986

ISBN 1 85190 013 6

First published June 1982
Second edition June 1986

© 1986 Fourmat Publishing
27 & 28 St Albans Place Islington Green London N1 0NX
Printed in Great Britain by
Billing & Sons Ltd., Worcester

Foreword

It was pleasing to be invited to write a second edition of this Practice and Procedure book, and I have taken the opportunity to expand many practice and procedure points, which have needed considerable up-dating since 1982. Because there is a specialist sister book on licensing, that subject has now been omitted, but a short chapter on traffic case practice added.

This book is still intended as a quick and easy guide for busy advocates in magistrates' courts, at the same time being of assistance to court clerks, prosecutors and magistrates. All should quickly get to the main provisions dealing with immediate practical problems.

Appendix 3 is new, and could usefully be ever immediately available in a courtroom. Judicial review, for changing mode of trial, plea and other matters would appear to be popular (with the Divisional Court and accused persons, if not with justices' clerks and the Lord Chancellor), and the charts are my own modest creation of a summary of the present position about mode of trial and plea, for instant use. Practice Directions are critical tools for use by advocates daily, and sometimes unexpectedly in costs applications. Advocates could probably quote them more often in court for better results, and they are here readily available.

With a book like this so much has to be left unwritten, and it is a fine judgement what to put in or leave out. I would like to think I have the balance right for the book to be helpful in the daily round, but I doubt it.

My grateful thanks are due to Valerie Phillips, my talented deputy, and David Gabbitass, both solicitors in Plymouth, from whom I have received great help. The mistakes are mine.

CHM
Plymouth, May 1986

Contents

Table of cases

List of abbreviations

AA 1976	Adoption Act 1976
AJA 1970	Administration of Justice Act 1970
APA 1957	Affiliation Proceedings Act 1957
BA 1976	Bail Act 1976
CA 1975	Children Act 1975
CCA 1980	Child Care Act 1980
CCCA 1973	Costs in Criminal Cases Act 1973
CCR 1971	Crown Court Rules 1971
CJA 1967	Criminal Justice Act 1967
CJA 1982	Criminal Justice Act 1982
CLA 1967	Criminal Law Act 1967
C&YPA 1933	Children & Young Persons Act 1933
C&YPA 1963	Children & Young Persons Act 1963
C&YPA 1969	Children & Young Persons Act 1969
DPMCA 1978	Domestic Proceedings and Magistrates' Courts Act 1978
GA 1973	Guardianship Act 1971
GLC(GP)A 1974	Greater London Council (General Powers) Act 1974
GMA 1971	Guardianship of Minors Act 1971
HA 1980	Highways Act 1980
LAA 1974	Legal Aid Act 1974
LAA 1979	Legal Aid Act 1979
LAA 1982	Legal Aid Act 1982
LA(G)R 1971	Legal Aid (General) Regulations 1971
MCA 1957	Magistrates' Courts Act 1957
MCA 1980	Magistrates' Courts Act 1980
MC(C&YP)R 1980	Magistrates' Courts (Children & Young Persons) Rules 1980
MC(F)R 1981	Magistrates' Courts (Forms) Rules 1981
MCR 1981	Magistrates' Courts Rules 1981
MFPA 1984	Matrimonial and Family Proceedings Act 1984
MP(MC)A 1960	Matrimonial Proceedings (Magistrates' Courts) Act 1960
PACEA 1984	Police & Criminal Evidence Act 1984
PCCA 1973	Powers of Criminal Courts Act 1973
POA 1985	Prosecution of Offences Act 1985

RSC 1965	Rules of the Supreme Court 1965
RTA 1972	Road Traffic Act 1972
RTRA 1984	Road Traffic Regulation Act 1984
TA 1968	Theft Act 1968
TA 1981	Transport Act 1981
TA 1982	Transport Act 1982
V(E)A 1971	Vehicles (Excise) Act 1971

Chapter 1

Introduction

1. Criminal jurisdiction

(a) Basic principles

The essence of the criminal process of magistrates' courts may be said to involve a person being *accused* of an *offence* which may or may not lead to his being *convicted* and *sentenced* for it. Proceedings are usually commenced either by the police charging a person with an offence or by the "laying" of an "information".

Magistrates' courts deal with more than 99% of all criminal cases at some stage either by summary trial, or by committal proceedings to the Crown Court.

The vast majority of criminal offences are created by statute, either specifically, eg Offences Against the Person Act 1861 and the Road Traffic Act 1972; or by regulations, breach of which is made an offence by statute, eg Motor Vehicles (Construction and Use) Regulations 1978 made under s.40(5) and Sched. 4 of the Road Traffic Act 1972, and Food Hygiene (General) Regulations 1970 made under ss.13 and 123 of the Food and Drugs Act 1955 (now Food Act 1984). But a few instances remain of criminal offences arising out of the common law, eg unlawful killing.

In criminal proceedings the burden of proof is always on the prosecution to prove the guilt of the accused person. The standard of proof is that of beyond reasonable doubt. In civil proceedings, by contrast, cases are decided on "a balance of probabilities".

(b) Terminology

Justices of the Peace are known as "justices" or "magistrates" in daily parlance. The statutes refer to *magistrates' courts*, and yet to *justices'* clerks. By custom and statute, Stipendiary Magistrates seem to keep the title "Magistrate", but lay justices retain the title "justices". There is no real significance in either user.

(c) Classification of offences

Offences coming before magistrates' courts fall into three categories:

(i) indictable offences, ie serious offences which, if committed by an adult are triable on indictment, ie at the Crown Court. There are two categories of such offence:

- *purely indictable offences*, which are the most serious criminal offences and are triable exclusively at the Crown Court, eg murder, rape;

- *either way offences*, which are serious offences but triable either at the Crown Court or magistrates' court, eg burglary, theft, reckless driving, etc. This class of offence includes those offences which may be triable summarily by reason of the value involved being small, eg criminal damage (MCA 1980 s.22).

(ii) *summary offences* — offences which if committed by an adult are triable only summarily, ie before a magistrates' court.

(d) Territorial jurisdiction

Indictable and either way offences: proceedings concerning indictable and either way offences may be commenced by the laying of an information (see page 9), before a justice of the peace or a justices' clerk, that a person has or is suspected of having committed an offence; hence proceedings for indictable offences or offences triable either way may be commenced anywhere in England and Wales regardless of local jurisdiction.

Summary offences: proceedings concerning summary offences may be commenced by the laying of an information in the same way; but the jurisdiction of the justices is limited to issuing process in respect of offences allegedly committed within the county or area only, or within 500 yards of the boundary. Summary proceedings may, however, be commenced in respect of an offence committed outside the county or area where:

(i) the alleged offender is charged *jointly* with or in the same place as another accused for whose alleged offence the justices already have jurisdiction; and

(ii) where a person is being tried for an offence before the justices in respect of which they already have jurisdiction.

Area means any county, a London Commission Area and the City of London. Counties are non-metropolitan (shire) or metropolitan. Even though the Local Government Act 1985 abolished the GLC and Metropolitan County Councils in 1986, each *area* remains and is the basis of a Commission of the Peace to which all justices must be appointed.

Summary proceedings may sometimes be commenced in the magistrates' court having jurisdiction in the place where the accused "is for the time being", or is residing when proceedings commence (see, eg Transport Act 1968 s.103(7)), but this is rare.

(e) Time limits

Indictable and either way offences: generally there is no time limit within which proceedings in respect of indictable offences have to be commenced, whether tried on indictment or summarily, but the particular statute creating the offence may itself stipulate a limitation, eg Sexual Offences Act 1956 s.37 and Sched. II(10); and the Trade Descriptions Act 1968 s.19, where a prosecution has to be brought within 3 years of the commission of the offence or one year from its discovery by the prosecutor, whichever is the earlier.

Summary offences: if the statute creating the offence contains no other restriction as to the time within which proceedings must be commenced, then the time prescribed by MCA 1980 s.127 will apply; the information must be laid within six months from the time when the offence was committed.

The information is laid at the time when the prosecutor brings the matter to the attention of the magistrates or justices' clerk (*R* v *Leeds Justices exp. Hanson (and other cases)* (1981)). The summons is issued on the day the information is placed before the justice or justices' clerk.

In calculating time, the day on which the offence was committed is not to be included.

In the case of a continuing offence which involves a new offence every day, the time limit runs from each day in turn.

2. Civil jurisdiction

(a) Basic principles

The character of the civil jurisdiction of magistrates' courts may, in simple terms, be stated to be that of affording persons who have suffered a wrong or who have a grievance to come to the court to seek a remedy against the wrongdoer. Proceedings are instituted by a person's making a *complaint* against a *defendant* or *respondent*, and the court's remedy is usually contained in an *order*.

The burden of proof in civil proceedings is, generally, upon he who makes the allegation or seeks the remedy; the standard of proof is on the preponderance of probabilities.

In both criminal and civil proceedings, if the burden of proving a fact ever "shifts" from the prosecutor or complainant to rest upon the defendant, the standard of proof then is on the balance of probabilities.

(b) Ambit of jurisdiction

The civil jurisdiction of magistrates' courts is governed by MCA 1980 ss.51 and 52, and encompasses such matters as:

  (i)   all domestic proceedings;
  (ii) all proceedings for the enforcement of debts (as opposed to fines), eg maintenance arrears enforceable as affiliation orders (see page 79) and rates enforceable as a civil debt;
  (iii) proceedings relating to dog orders;
  (iv) proceedings relating to orders of binding over;
  (v)   proceedings relating to abatement of nuisance orders;
  (vi) proceedings relating to care proceedings in the juvenile court.

In some old statutes words like "complaint" and "information" were used indiscriminately; MCA 1980 s.50 has enacted that whenever an Act confers a power on a magistrates' court to deal with an offence on the "complaint" of any person, for references to a "complaint" there shall be substituted references to an "information".

(c) Territorial jurisdiction

A magistrates' court has jurisdiction to hear a complaint if it relates to an act or omission or other matter arising within the commission area (ie every county, London commission area and the City of London) for which the court is appointed.

(d) Time limitation

The time or period within which civil proceedings may be instituted is governed as in criminal matters by MCA 1980 s.127. The comments on page 3 apply equally to civil proceedings as to criminal proceedings.

3. Juveniles

The jurisdiction of the juvenile court is confined strictly to the matters which are assigned to it by statute; see C&YPA 1933 s.46.

Before proceedings are taken against juveniles, regard must be had to the age of the offender:

(i) it is conclusively presumed that no child under 10 years of age can be guilty of any offence;

(ii) a child under the age of 14 years is presumed not to know the difference between right and wrong and therefore to be incapable of committing offences, but the presumption may be rebutted by strong evidence of criminal propensity;

(iii) the incapacity of children to commit crime ceases upon their attaining the age of 14 years, at which age they are presumed by law to be capable of appreciating their criminal actions.

4. Practical considerations

Before instituting any proceedings, whether civil or criminal, it is suggested that enquiries be made of the office of the clerk to the justices who operates within the court area. Information can then be given as to the local geographical areas covered by the petty sessional division. Liaison is also necessary regarding the arrangements for the actual laying of an information and whether a personal attendance is required; and the times when attendances are convenient. A date may also have to be fixed for the hearing, which can only be given by the office of the justices' clerk. It is important that precise information relating to the person initiating the proceedings and the defendant to them is available; the forms of information or complaint which may be used for the proceedings may be obtained from some law publishers as well as from the clerk to the justices.

The police keep records of some convictions to produce at court in connection with their own prosecutions. In any criminal proceedings the non-police prosecutor may wish to liaise with the local police force to arrange for previous convictions recorded against the accused to be produced at the hearing. Free access to this information is of course prohibited and local arrangements differ as to how such information is made available.

If it is intended to cite previous convictions at the hearing in the event of the accused being convicted and being absent, notice of such particulars must have been served on the accused not less than seven days before the hearing, otherwise they cannot be mentioned.

Chapter 2

Instituting criminal proceedings

1. Who may prosecute

In practice most criminal proceedings are brought by the police, but anyone may prosecute for a criminal offence unless the relevant statute contains any limitation, eg:

    (i) Customs and Excise Management Act 1979: prosecutions can only be brought by the Customs and Excise authorities;

    (ii) Offences Against the Person Act 1961 s.42: only injured parties may commence assault proceedings;

    (iii) Public Health Act 1936 s.298: without the consent of the Attorney General only the party aggrieved may institute proceedings in respect of an offence created by the Act.

Proceedings are commenced either by laying an information or by arrest and charge.

A local authority instituted proceedings by one of their own solicitors, authorised to do so. It was argued that under the Shops Act 1950 the authority had no power to proceed through their solicitor and that the proceedings should have been instituted by an Inspector appointed under the Act. It was held that their own solicitor could begin proceedings, and they were not bound to use one of their inspectors to prosecute (*Wickes Building Supplies Limited* v *Kirklees Metropolitan District Council* (1984) 148 JP 106).

2. Crown Prosecution Service

Under the Prosecution of Offences Act 1985, there is created a Crown Prosecution Service, headed by the Director of Public

Prosecutions ("DPP"). This came into operation on 1 April 1986 in Durham, Greater Manchester, Merseyside, Northumberland, South Yorkshire, Tyne and Wear, West Midlands and West Yorkshire (to coincide with the abolition of the Metropolitan County Councils), and is operative in the rest of the country from 1 October 1986.

(a) The Crown Prosecutors

Under the DPP there will be several regional Chief Crown Prosecutors, and then several hundred Crown Prosecutors, who will be responsible for the conduct of all criminal proceedings in England and Wales, other than specified proceedings, instituted on behalf of a police force. In addition, whoever might otherwise be the prosecutor, the Crown Prosecution Service will be able to institute and conduct criminal proceedings where they are important or difficult, or where for any other reason it is appropriate for the Crown Prosecutor to be involved. There are functions to take over other prosecutions, and, importantly, to give advice to police forces on matters relating to criminal offences.

These Crown Prosecutors will have the same rights of audience enjoyed by solicitors in any court, and any additional rights in the Crown Court which might be given to them. Crown Prosecutors will all be solicitors or barristers. Non-Crown prosecutors, solicitors or barristers, might be appointed by the DPP to take over the conduct of criminal cases, and shall be deemed to be Crown Prosecutors with one or two restrictions. All Crown Prosecutors will have the powers of the DPP for the institution and conduct of proceedings, but will be under DPP direction.

Any private prosecution can be taken over by the DPP at any time. Private prosecutions begun and not proceeded with within a reasonable time will lead to the justices' clerk sending the papers to the DPP if the justices' clerk suspects there is no satisfactory reason for withdrawal of the case or failure to proceed.

(b) Code of Conduct

There will be a Code of Conduct for Crown Prosecutors issued by the DPP. It will give general guidance on the principles to be applied in the following matters:

(i) determining whether proceedings shall be instituted;

(ii) where proceedings have been instituted (by the police, often), determining whether they should be discontinued;

(iii) deciding what charges should be preferred;

(iv) the representations that should be made by the prosecution to magistrates' courts about mode of trial
suitable in any given case.

(c) Time when proceedings are instituted

To add another dimension to the thorny problem of when
proceedings commence (see page 16), for the purposes of the DPP
being involved, proceedings are instituted:

(i)   where a justice of the peace or justices' clerk issues a
summons, when the information for the offence is laid
before him;
(ii) where a justice of the peace issues a warrant for the arrest
of any person, when the information for the offence is laid
before him;
(iii) where a person is charged with the offence after being
taken into custody without a warrant, when he is informed
of the particulars of the charge;
(iv) when a bill of indictment is preferred direct to the Crown
Court (the only time when a case can be heard at the
Crown Court without going through the magistrates'
court).

(d) Other provisions

There is provision for Regulations to be made to avoid undue delay
in criminal proceedings. Regulations could fix time limits for the
various stages from arrest through committal proceedings to trial at
a Crown Court. It is interesting to note that where there are time
limits, time does not run when a prisoner escapes from custody!

Section 23 provides that, in certain circumstances, the DPP may
give notice that he does not want the proceedings to continue, and
then those proceedings shall be discontinued forthwith. Reasons
have to be given. Optimistically, the statute makes provision for an
accused to *require* the proceedings to be continued, even when the
DPP does not want that to happen. But it could be used to clear an
accused's name if he felt strongly about it and wanted a formal
acquittal. Peculiarly, the discontinuance of any criminal proceedings does not prevent the institution of fresh proceedings in respect
of the same offence.

3. Laying an information

(a) Content and form of information

An information can be oral, but is mostly in writing; it is simply the statement by which the justice is informed of the alleged offence. A form of information is reproduced at page 129. The information must state:

(i) the name of the person charged;

(ii) the alleged offence;

(iii) the date when the offence was allegedly committed;

(iv) the place where the offence was allegedly committed.

In many courts the same printed form is used for both an information and the summons.

"It is sensible to treat an unsigned copy of the summons as the information." (*per* Griffiths LJ in *R* v *Leeds Justices ex parte Hanson* (1981) (see page 3)).

(b) Statement of offence

The offence should be described in the information clearly and definitely without duplicity or uncertainty; it is sufficient to use the words of the statute, which itself should be cited, especially a local statute. But:

(i) where the offence contains a defence involving an exception or proviso etc (which may be contained in the words of the creating statute) it is not necessary for the wording of the information to negative the exception or proviso;

(ii) a variance between the time and place stated and that proved will not be material if it is proved in evidence that the prosecution commenced within the period prescribed and that the offence was committed within the jurisdiction of the court by which the information is heard and determined (MCA 1980 ss.1 – 3, 123). But if a defendant is misled about a variation between the offence alleged and the evidence actually adduced, the court must adjourn the hearing if asked. Where justices found a theft was committed later than alleged, that was a slight variation and did no injustice (*Creek* v *Peck & Jones* (1983));

(iii) where the date cannot be accurately stated the informant may allege the offence to have been committed between stated dates. Incorrect spelling of the accused's name is not fatal if *idem sonans* or if he appears to the summons;

(iv) incorrect recital of ownership in the information or of the date of the offence may be rectified by an amendment of the information or adjournment — the case should not be dismissed;

(v) if the wrong person is summoned, eg the secretary of a limited company instead of the company (see page 16), the information is bad;

(vi) an information which alleges the commission of a continuing offence on more than one day is bad for duplicity as a continuing offence involves a new offence arising every day;

(vii) no objection is to be allowed to any information, summons or warrant for any alleged defect in substance or form (MCA 1980 s.123).

(c) Joinder of offenders

Several alleged offenders may be joined in one information if the act complained of admits the participation of several persons.

(d) Several offences

The information must be for one offence only (MCR 1981 r.12). Where an information alleges more than a single offence the prosecutor should be called upon before the trial commences to decide on which offence he desires the court to proceed; and when this selection has been made the other offence or offences should be struck out. If the prosecutor refuses, the information is bad and the court should dismiss it. But this should be contrasted with an allegation of being in charge of a motor vehicle whilst under the influence of drink or drugs, which is not bad for uncertainty because the essence of the offence is being *in charge* of the motor vehicle while in a state of incapacity.

The words "aiding and abetting, counselling and procuring" constitute one offence.

There is nothing objectionable in one or more informations being set out in one document. However, if there is one common preamble, followed by multiple offences, this is not acceptable. Multiple offences on one document must be separately stated *in full* (*R* v *Brigg Justices, ex parte Lynch* (1984)).

(e) Formalities

The information may be oral and unsworn in the case of a request for a summons, but must be in writing and on oath in the case of a warrant. Subject to this, and any other contrary statutory provision, it may be laid by the prosecutor in person or by his counsel or solicitor, or other person authorised in that behalf.

(f) Issue of summonses and warrants after laying information

A justice or a justices' clerk before whom an information is laid may issue a summons, addressed to the defendant. As mentioned above, the information and summons may follow the same form. The summons must:

(i) be signed by the justice issuing it or state his name and be authenticated by the signature of the clerk to the justices;

(ii) state shortly the matter of the information; and

(iii) state the time and place at which the defendant is required by the summons to appear at court.

A single summons may be issued against a person in respect of several informations, but the summons must state the matter of each information separately. This has the same effect as if separate summonses had been issued.

Note that summonses are *served* on people by giving them a copy. But warrants (of arrest or of commitment to prison) are *executed*. The words "served" and "executed" are regularly improperly exchanged, sometimes by the press.

A warrant is often issued in serious cases or where the offender is unlikely to attend as a result of a summons. In the case of adults, however, the power to issue a warrant in the first instance is confined to:

(i) indictable offences;

(ii) offences punishable with imprisonment;

(iii) cases where the address of the offender is not sufficiently established for a summons to be served upon him.

The effect of a warrant is that a police constable is authorised to arrest the alleged offender and take him into custody. Warrants (except where alleging treason) may be "backed for bail", so that once arrested the alleged offender may be released on bail to appear at the magistrates' court at a time and place specified, with or without sureties. Warrants may be executed anywhere in England or Wales by any person to whom directed or by any constable acting within his police area. They remain in force until executed or withdrawn, despite the death of the issuing justice. Any warrant issued by a justice may be executed at any time including Sunday. Requirements as to their content, signature and execution are contained in MCR 1981 rr.94–96. Warrants, with some exceptions, can be executed in Scotland, Northern Ireland, the Isle of Man and the Channel Islands.

4. Charge after arrest

As an alternative to commencing proceedings by information, the criminal process may be initiated by the arrest of a person:

(i) by a private individual under PACEA 1984 s.24(4), and

(ii) by a constable under PACEA 1984 s.24(6).

In this instance proceedings are commenced when the accused is formally charged; usually at a police station in front of what will now be a "custody officer" (see below).

Very wide powers of arrest are now given to the police to arrest for quite minor non-arrestable offences, where the police think the service of a summons impracticable or inappropriate (PACEA 1984 s.25).

(a) Arrest without warrant

Any person may arrest without warrant:

(i) anyone who is in the act of committing an arrestable offence;

(ii) anyone whom he has reasonable grounds for suspecting to be committing such an offence.

Where an arrestable offence *has* been committed, any person may arrest without warrant:

(i) anyone who is guilty of the offence;

(ii) anyone whom he has reasonable grounds for suspecting to be guilty of it

(PACEA 1984 s.24).

Where a constable has reasonable grounds for suspecting that an arrestable offence has been committed he may arrest without warrant anyone whom he has reasonable grounds for suspecting to be guilty of the offence.

A constable may arrest without warrant:

(i) anyone who is about to commit an arrestable offence;

(ii) anyone whom he has reasonable grounds for suspecting to be about to commit an arrestable offence;

(iii) anyone breaching the peace, or obstructing him in the execution of his duty.

Arrestable offences in respect of which there is a general power to arrest without warrant, independent of any specific authority, are defined in PACEA 1984 s.24 and Sched. 2 as:

(i) offences for which the sentence is fixed by law (eg murder);

(ii) offences punishable for an adult by 5 years' imprisonment;

(iii) certain offences against the Customs and Excise Acts or Official Secrets Acts, sexual offences against women, taking motor vehicles and corruption charges, including conspiracy, attempting, inciting and aiding them;

(iv) Sched. 2 — a "preserved" list of rarely charged offences.

Other powers of arrest without warrant are given, *inter alia*, to constables under the Town Police Clauses Act 1847; and to constables employed by the British Railways Board in respect of persons committing offences on the Board's property.

(b) After charging

A person arrested and charged with an offence without warrant and not bailed, must be taken before a court as soon as practicable; and in any event not later than the first sitting after he is charged, normally the day after the charge, except for Sundays, Christmas Day and Good Friday (PACEA 1984 s.46).

5. Commencing criminal proceedings against juveniles

See page 5 as to the criminal responsibility of juveniles.

(a) By information

Informations may be laid against juveniles (10–16 years inclusive) in the same way as adults; the same considerations and restrictions apply, but the following are additional:

(i) *attendance at court of parents:* where a juvenile is charged with any offence, or is for any other reason brought before the court, any parent or guardian of his may be, and commonly is, required to attend at the court with the juvenile, and a summons or warrant may be issued to compel the appearance of any parent at the court;

(ii) *notice to social agencies:* any person who decides to lay an information alleging an offence:

- ● must, where the alleged offender is a juvenile, give notice of that decision to the local authority in whose area the juvenile resides (C&YPA 1969 s.5(8)); and in addition

- ● give notice of the decision to a probation officer for the area for which the court acts.

(b) By arrest and charge

The powers of arrest without warrant apply equally to juveniles as they do to adults, except that a juvenile must be fairly quickly taken into the care of a local authority, unless the police custody officer certifies it impracticable and if the juvenile is not granted bail (PACEA 1984 s.38).

(c) Juvenile court's jurisdiction

Juvenile court summonses and warrants against juveniles must direct them to attend the juvenile court; and juveniles charged with offences must appear before the juvenile court.

The adult court *may* deal with juveniles:

(i) charged with aiding and abetting an adult; or

(ii) where the offence arose out of circumstances which are the same as or connected with those giving rise to an offence with which an adult is charged at the same time.

The adult court *must* hear an information against a juvenile jointly charged with an adult (C&YPA 1933 s.46(1); C&YPA 1963 s.18), and not otherwise; but:

(i) where a defendant is discovered to be a juvenile only in the course of proceedings in the adult court, the court may continue nevertheless;

(ii) the restrictions on the jurisdiction of the adult court do not prevent it from hearing a remand application;

(iii) where a child or young person is proceeded against and "convicted" under the guilty plea by letter procedure

(MCA 1980 s.12) in the adult court rather than the juvenile court, he shall be deemed to have attained the age of 17 years for the purposes of those proceedings.

(See also page 50).

These provisions are most complex, yet vitally important by virtue of the sentencing options open in different courts.

6. Proceedings against corporations

Corporations may be offenders and fined; and informations may be laid against them as above, but:

(i) any information or summons should be addressed to the company, not to the secretary or other officer;

(ii) the secretary or other officer authorised may acknowledge;

(iii) the company's address can be its registered office or other address from which it trades in England or Wales.

7. When do proceedings commence?

The point at which proceedings are commenced is determined by whether they are instituted by laying an information or by arrest and charge; and whether the accused is a juvenile. This point can be crucial when Parliament changes maximum penalties or abolishes offences.

(a) Adults

The date proceedings are commenced when an information is laid is the date when the contents are brought to the attention of a justice, or the clerk to the justices, as part of the prosecution process. The date of issue of the summons here is irrelevant (*R* v *Leeds JJ ex parte Hanson* (1981)).

When proceedings are commenced by arrest and charge, the date when the accused is charged with the offence at the police station is the date when proceedings are taken to commence, not when he appears before the court (*R* v *Brentwood JJ ex parte Jones* (1979)).

(b) Juveniles

Compared with the position in relation to adults, the question of when proceedings against juveniles commence is anomolous.

It must be remembered that the age of an accused child or young person may, at the early stages of proceedings, determine his options as to right of jury trial, as well as the penalties which the court can inflict if he is found guilty; and he can to some degree arrange affairs to his advantage. Proceedings are begun, it seems, when the juvenile first "appears" before the court:

By information: In the case of *R* v *Billericay JJ ex parte Johnson* (1979) Widgery LCJ held that proceedings are begun when the offender is summoned to appear before the court, ie not with the laying of the information, but with the actual service of the summons. It follows, therefore, that if service of the summons cannot be effected for a period, adult court proceedings may become possible through passage of time (and see *R* v *St. Albans Juvenile Court ex parte Godman* (1981)).

By arrest and charge: in *R* v *Amersham Juvenile Court ex parte Wilson* (1981), C&YPA 1963 s.29 was considered. This section provides that where proceedings in respect of a young person are begun for an offence and he attains the age of 17 before the conclusion of the proceedings, the court may deal with the case and make any order which it could have made if he had not attained that age. It was held that where an offender attains 17 years during the period between arrest and charge, and appearance in court, proceedings are commenced when he first appears or is brought before a court. His age is fixed and he therefore ceases to be a juvenile, so that the date of commencement of proceedings where a juvenile offender is arrested and charged is the date he first appears or is brought before the court. But see *R* v *Islington North Juvenile Court, ex parte Daley* (1982).

The later case of *R* v *Lewes Juvenile Court, ex parte Turner* (1985) tidies up somewhat. The crucial ages are 16 or 17 years, with, normally, summary trial *only* for the 16 year old (and juvenile court); the 17-year old has an option for jury trial (in the adult court with increased possible penalties). The material date is the date the mode of trial decision was made, so, if a 16-year old pleads guilty or not guilty, and the case is then adjourned to a date by which he has attained 17, he does not have the jury trial option.

Chapter 3

Instituting civil proceedings

1. Making the complaint

A complaint may be made to a justice of the peace or a justices' clerk acting in any petty sessions in which a magistrates' court acting for that area has power to make an order against any person.

As in the case of the laying of an information in criminal proceedings, the justice or clerk hearing the application for a summons to be issued acts judicially; but a complaint may be made, and the issuing of the summons delayed, eg when the whereabouts of the respondent are not known but the complaint needs to be made within a time limit, eg as required by MCA 1980 s.127.

2. Who may institute proceedings

The complaint, which need not generally be in written form nor on oath, may be made by the complainant in person or by his counsel or solicitor, or other person authorised in that behalf (MCR 1981 r.4).

3. Care proceedings in the juvenile court

(a) Civil proceedings

Care proceedings are civil proceedings and as such are regulated by MCA 1980 Part II. The institution and conduct of care proceedings are provided for in C&YPA 1969 ss.1 and 2 and MC(C&YP)R 1980 Part III.

(b) Who may institute proceedings

Any local authority, constable or authorised person (see below) who

18

reasonably believes that there are grounds for making an order in respect of a child or young person may bring him before a juvenile court (C&YPA 1969 s.1). In fact, every local authority is under a *duty* to bring care proceedings in respect of a child if there appear to be grounds for so doing; and although a parent or guardian cannot himself bring care proceedings, he may make a written request to the local authority to do so.

The NSPCC is the only other "authorised person" who may bring care proceedings under this provision (C&YPA 1969 s.1(2)).

Notice of the proceedings must be given to the local authority for the area in which it appears the juvenile resides; and to the probation officer for the area if the juvenile is 12 years or over (see page 15).

(c) Grounds for bringing care proceedings

The grounds for which the above bodies or persons can institute proceedings are contained in C&YPA 1969 s.1. These are called the "primary conditions":

(i) the proper development of the child or young person is being avoidably prevented or neglected or his health is being avoidably impaired, or he is being ill-treated; or

(ii) that the court, or any other court, has found that a condition mentioned in (i) above is or was satisfied in the case of another child or young person, who is or was a member of the same household and that it will probably be satisfied in his case also. The dominant factor is the persons who comprise the household and not the place where the household is located (see *N (a Minor)* v *Birmingham District Council* (1984)); or

(iii) it is probable that the condition mentioned in (i) above will be satisfied because a person who has been convicted of an offence mentioned in C&YPA 1933 Sched 1 is or may become a member of the same household as the child; or

(iv) he is exposed to moral danger; or

(v) he is beyond the control of his parent; or

(vi) he is of compulsory school age and is not receiving efficient suitable full time education; or

(vii) he (not under 10) is guilty of an offence, excluding homicide.

Note: Proceedings under ground (vi) above can be instituted by a local education authority only; proceedings under (vii) by the local authority or a constable only (s.1(2)). But where a constable brings proceedings, they can only proceed if the DPP has consented to the allegation being made (POA 1985 s.27, when in force).

(d) Ambit of care proceedings

Any proceedings brought in the juvenile court under the general wording of "care proceedings" include proceedings brought, or proposed to be brought, for:

(i)   care proceedings under C&YPA 1969 s.1;

(ii) variation and discharge of supervision orders under s.15;

(iii) variation and discharge of care orders under s.21;

(iv) variation of supervision to Scotland under Sched. 4 para. 2.

(e) Unopposed applications

In any unopposed application (called a "Maria Colwell case") for the discharge of a supervision order or care order made in "care proceedings", the court is prevented by C&YPA 1969 s.32A from treating any parent or guardian as representing the child. Hence a guardian *ad litem* may be required to be appointed under MC(C&YP)R 1980 r.14A. Inquiry should be made at an early stage of the proceedings, initially of the clerk of the court, for directions as to the necessity for and the appointment of such a guardian *ad litem*.

(f) Process in care proceedings

A juvenile may be brought before the court in care proceedings as follows:

(i)   voluntarily without the issue of any process;

(ii) by summons, or if he does not respond to a summons or a summons cannot be served, by a warrant (C&YPA 1969 s.2(4));

(iii) by a warrant where it can be shown that he is being assaulted or ill-treated, neglected, or subjected to the commission of certain offences (C&YPA 1933 s.40);

(iv) following detention under a place of safety order (see *(j)* below);

(v) following detention by a constable under C&YPA 1969 s.28(c) (see *(k)* below).

Note: It is not free from doubt whether a warrant may be issued without a summons having first been served or an attempt at service made. The power to issue warrants in civil cases is severely limited (MCA 1980 s.55).

(g) Respondents

Where care proceedings are commenced otherwise than by summons, the applicant must notify the persons mentioned in MC(C&YP)R 1980 r.14, the most important of whom are:

(i) the clerk of the court;

(ii) the relevant infant;

(iii) the parents or guardian of the relevant infant;

(iv) any foster parent or other person with whom the infant has had his home for a period of not less than six weeks within the preceding 27 weeks;

(v) the appropriate local authority.

(h) Contents of notice

The notice which must be sent, and which is usually addressed to the clerk of the court, must contain the following information:

(i) the grounds upon which the proceedings are brought;

(ii) the names and addresses of the persons to whom a copy of the notice is sent;

(iii) the date, time and place appointed for the hearing.

In any application for the discharge of a supervision order or care order made in care proceedings, any such notice sent to persons other than the clerk of the court, must be accompanied by a notice stating that the recipient should inform the clerk of the court as soon as practicable and not later than 14 days after its receipt by him, whether or not he intends to oppose the application. See the decision at page 56-57.

(i) Commencement of proceedings by summons

The steps to be followed leading to issue of a summons for care proceedings are the same as in other civil proceedings; see page 18.

(j) Commencement of proceedings following place of safety order

Under C&YPA 1969 s.28(1), where a justice of the peace is satisfied that the applicant has reasonable cause to believe, *inter alia*, that any of the primary conditions of s.1 is satisfied with respect to the juvenile, except the offence condition, he may make an order authorising the juvenile to be detained and taken to a place of safety. There is no limitation on the persons who may apply for such an order, but if care proceedings follow, they may only be brought by someone who is statutorily entitled to do so. Such applications may be made *ex parte* and are used in emergencies. Liaison with the justices' clerk is recommended before a justice of the peace is contacted.

The justice may make an order in this case for a period of 28 days beginning with the date of the order, or for a shorter period as may be specified in the order. Seven days is not uncommon, and indeed was recommended as a maximum by the Beckford Report (see The Times 4 December 1985).

The person making the application should have regard to the date of the next juvenile court sitting in the area, and the length of time necessary to serve notices or summonses (under *(h)* and *(i)* above).

It should be remembered that the justice granting an application under this provision will have regard to the fact that the order is made *ex parte* and that the parents or guardian should have a right to be heard as soon as reasonably practicable.

(k) Commencement of proceedings following detention by a police constable

Under C&YPA 1969 s.28(2), any constable may detain any juvenile in respect of whom he has reasonable cause to believe that any of the primary conditions of s.1, except the offence condition or the education condition, is satisfied.

Any constable acting under this section may detain the juvenile in a place of safety for up to eight days and an application for an interim care order may be made under s.28 following the juvenile's detention.

4. Local authority's assumption of parental rights

(a) By resolution

Section 3, CCA 1980 provides that a local authority who has a child in its care under s.2 of the Act may resolve that there shall vest in it the parental rights and duties with respect to that child, if it appears that one of nine conditions contained in s.3 of the Act applies.

Unless consent has been given by the person whose parental rights and duties have vested in the local authority by virtue of the resolution, the local authority gives written notice of the passing of the resolution to any person whose rights and duties are affected; such notice must:

(i) be given forthwith;

(ii) inform the person of his right to object to the resolution and the effect of any objection made by him; and

(iii) be served by registered or recorded delivery post.

(b) Counter notice

Under CCA 1980 s.3(4), a person upon whom a notice of assumption of parental rights has been served may serve a counter notice which will have the effect of causing the resolution to lapse on the expiry of fourteen days from the service of the counter notice, subject as follows:

(i) the counter notice must be served upon the local authority not later than one month from the date the notice of assumption of parental rights is served upon the parent;

(ii) the counter notice must give notice that the parent objects to the assumption of parental rights;

(iii) service of the notice may be by ordinary post, but it is recommended that registered or recorded delivery post be used.

(c) Complaints to a juvenile court

Where the counter notice has been served on the local authority, the authority may not take more than fourteen days after receipt by them of the counter notice to complain to a juvenile court having jurisdiction in the area of the authority, whereupon the resolution does not lapse until the determination of the complaint (CCA 1980 s.3(5)).

The complaint must be made to a juvenile court, not simply to a justice of the peace. Procedure thereafter will be in accordance with the institution of any civil proceedings.

Legal aid may be granted under the Legal Aid (Extension of

Proceedings) Regulations 1969, by application to a local committee of The Law Society, to a person who objects to or takes proceedings to determine a resolution by the local authority to assume parental rights.

Chapter 4

In Court: criminal proceedings

1. Before charge

With the advent of PACEA 1984, persons who are suspected of having committed serious arrestable offences (defined in s.116) may be detained in police custody, with certain safeguards, for up to 36 hours *without charge*. If the police desire detention over and above that, they must get permission from a magistrates' court under s.43. A magistrates' court may authorise further detention only if:

(a) the detention without charge is necessary to secure or preserve evidence relating to the offence for which the suspect is under arrest, or to obtain such evidence by questioning him; and

(b) the investigation is being conducted diligently and expeditiously.

The magistrates' court can authorise the suspect to be kept in police detention for a period no longer than 36 hours, by one or more orders, but so long as the overall period from arrest to that authorized, shall not exceed 96 hours. The suspect is entitled to legal representation on that hearing. Any detention over 36 hours by a magistrates' court shall be ordered by a warrant of further detention. The court need not be open court.

2. Jurisdiction to deal with charges etc

MCA 1980 s.2 provides authority to justices to deal with charges — this is in effect the same jurisdiction as justices have to issue process; see page 12.

If justices decline jurisdiction to hear an information, the appropriate remedy is an appeal by way of case stated (see page 115) and not judicial review (*R* v *Clerkenwell Metropolitan Stipendiary Magistrates ex parte DPP* (1984)).

3. Modes of trial

There are two modes of trial in English law; trial on indictment and summary trial. The first takes place at the Crown Court, the second at a magistrates' court, but for the purposes of ascertaining how they are to be tried, *offences* can be divided into three categories:

(a) *offences triable only on indictment*, where the function of the magistrates' court is solely the holding of a preliminary enquiry or committal proceedings, the actual trial taking place at the Crown Court;

(b) *offences triable only summarily*, where the magistrates' court has exclusive jurisdiction; these offences cannot be tried at the Crown Court;

(c) *offences triable either way*, either at the Crown Court or in a magistrates' court after the justices have heard representations from the parties as to which mode of trial is appropriate and have decided. But always the accused himself may claim jury trial as a right. There is only one exception to that rule. An accused may claim his right to jury trial, but if it turns out he is mentally ill, to such an extent the court might make a Hospital Order (s.37(3), Mental Health Act 1983), then without a conviction, and with no trial at the Crown Court, that order can be made by magistrates. It remains to be decided whether this applies to a purely indictable offence at (a) above (*R* v *Ramsgate Justices ex parte Kazmarek* (1985)).

4. Committal proceedings

A committal for trial on indictment in respect of an offence triable exclusively on indictment, or either on indictment or summarily, is regulated by MCA 1980 ss.4–8, 28, 41 & 102; as well as MCR 1981. There are two methods of committal for trial:

(a) committal by consent of the accused without consideration of the evidence by the court; and

(b) committal after full enquiry or after reception of evidence, which might be oral or written statements or both.

Committal proceedings are generally conducted in open court, and may be heard by a single justice; any justice or justices so sitting are called examining justices. Before beginning to enquire into an offence as examining justices, or at any time during the inquiry, the court may adjourn the hearing and, in such cases, must remand the accused, in custody or on bail (see page 40).

The standard of proof in committal proceedings is for the prosecution to satisfy the court that there is sufficient evidence against the accused for him to stand his trial at the Crown Court, ie there must be a *prima facie* case.

(a) Committal proceedings by consent — without considering evidence (MCA 1980 s.6(2)).

Where examining justices are satisfied that certain conditions have been met, the accused may be committed for trial to the Crown Court without consideration by them of evidence or statements of evidence. The conditions are that:

(i) the charge is in written form, and has been read to the accused at the hearing;

(ii) all the evidence before the court, whether of the prosecution or defence, consists of written statements (conforming to conditions contained in MCA 1980 s.102) with or without exhibits, copies of which have been given to the accused;

(iii) each of the accused is legally represented by counsel or a solicitor;

(iv) there is no objection by or on behalf of the accused to any of the prosecution statements being tendered in evidence;

(v) there is no submission by or on behalf of the accused that the statements do not disclose a *prima facie* case against him; and

(vi) there is to be no evidence called by or on behalf of the accused.

If any of these conditions is not met, the proceedings must take the form of committal in *(b)* below. Where all the above conditions *are* satisfied, the court may then commit the accused for trial.

(b) Committal proceedings: full inquiry

Committal proceedings conducted otherwise than by consent of the accused are regulated by MCA 1980 s.6(1) and MCR 1981 r.7.

27

Sometimes the prosecution may elect to call all their witnesses to give evidence; or may adduce their evidence entirely by written statements, which must usually be read out; or by a mixture of both. Both the defence and prosecution are able to cross examine any witness called by the other side.

The procedure at the hearing is regulated by MCR 1981 r.7, which provides that:

(i)   all evidence given by witnesses, including that of the accused, is to be written down (usually typewritten) as a deposition, read over to the witness and signed by him;

(ii)   all depositions are to be certificated by one of the examining justices;

(iii)   where the accused is unrepresented, and evidence of a child relating to a sexual offence is to be given, the court must explain that a written statement by the child may be admissible as evidence, which is then made an exhibit;

(iv)   at the conclusion of the prosecution case, a submission by the defence may be made following which the court decides either:

- to discharge the accused (in which case the proceedings are concluded subject to any ancillary applications as to costs, legal aid etc);
- that there is sufficient evidence for the accused to answer, whereupon:

(v)   the charge must be put into written form if this has not been done already, and read to the accused, and he must be asked whether he wishes to say anything in answer to it.

If he is unrepresented, however, before asking him, the court must inform him that he may give evidence and call witnesses, or remain silent; but in so doing the accused must be reminded that any statement or evidence will be recorded, and he must not be influenced by any promises or threats;

(vi)   whatever the accused says in answer to the charge must be written down, read over to him and signed by one of the examining justices, and also by the accused if he wishes;

(vii)   the accused may call witnesses and give evidence himself;

(viii)   the legal representative of the accused may address the court either before or after the defence evidence is given, and with the leave of the court before *and* after, but in this event, the prosecution may also address the court;

(ix) as in para (iv) above, after hearing all the evidence, the court will either discharge the accused or commit him to the Crown Court for trial.

Where the court decides to commit the accused for trial in respect of a charge differing from that read to him at para (v) above, the court shall cause the new charge to be written down and be read to him.

When examining justices find there is no *prima facie* case for an (only) indictable offence, but there is for a (lesser) either way offence, they cannot revert to summary trial and must commit for trial on the lesser offence (*R* v *Cambridge Justices, ex parte Fraser* (1984)).

(c) Attendance of the accused

Except in the case of disorderly conduct or, with certain savings, ill health, all committal proceedings must be conducted in the presence of the accused.

The court is not concerned with the circumstances in which the accused was found within the jurisdiction so long as he is there. An Australian was suspected of murder in England, and went to Turkey; there the authorities arrested him and put him on an aeroplane for England where he was arrested. There was no extradition treaty with Turkey. The committal was to continue (*R* v *Plymouth Magistrates' Court and Others, ex parte Driver* (1985)).

(d) Press restrictions on committal proceedings

In committal proceedings the press are allowed to report no more than certain prescribed formalities, unless the court makes an order removing the restrictions. The formal matters which may be published are contained in MCA 1980 s.8(4) and include, eg:

(i) the identity of the court, and names of the justices;
(ii) the names, addresses and occupations of the parties and witnesses and their respective ages;
(iii) the offence, or offences alleged, or a summary of them.

The press restrictions above shall be lifted at any stage of the proceedings on an application by the accused, or one of the accused; but where there are two or more accused, and one only objects to the lifting of restrictions, the restrictions may be lifted only if the court considers it is in the interests of justice to do so (Criminal Justice (Amendment) Act 1981). Any application to allow full reporting of the proceedings must therefore be shown to be for the benefit of the trial, not for personal gain. The paramount consideration is a fair trial. A powerful case is needed to overcome the general rule of no reporting (*R* v *Leeds Justices, ex parte Sykes* (1983)).

A number of other restrictions on publicity should also be noted:

(i)   restrictions imposed on the press under this section will not override other provisions regulating publicity contained in other legislation, eg C&YPA 1969; Sexual Offences (Amendment) Act 1976; Contempt of Court Act 1981 (to protect juveniles or rape "victims" from publicity, mostly);

(ii) the identification of the injured party *and* the accused is restricted by the Sexual Offences Amendment Act 1976; the restriction may, on application, be lifted by the court for an accused;

(iii) restrictions on reporting committal proceedings exist only during their continuation; on discharging the accused the press are entitled to publish full details.

(e) Alibi warning

At the conclusion of the proceedings the accused must usually be given an opportunity to give notice (within 7 days) of the fact that he proposes at his trial to raise a defence of alibi; such defence evidence may not be allowed at a trial unless notice has been given to the prosecution within stated time limits.

(f) Witnesses

Witnesses at committal proceedings, including those whose evidence is in written statement form, must be made subject of an order to attend the trial; the order may or may not be conditional upon their being given notice to attend. Prosecution and defence representatives usually indicate to the court which witnesses are required to attend absolutely or conditionally. If the plea at trial is likely to be guilty, then the witness order would be conditional to attend for a possible not guilty plea.

There is no necessity for an accused to give evidence himself in order to be entitled to call witnesses in his defence, in full committal proceedings. Rule 7(10) of MCR 1981 provides that "the court shall give the accused an opportunity to give evidence himself and to call witnesses". That should not be read conjunctively and r.6(2) makes clear the fundamental rights of an accused *not* to give evidence, but to call witnesses on his behalf, if he wishes (*R* v *Blyth Valley Justices ex parte Fawcus* (1986)).

(g) Exhibits

Any exhibits produced at the hearing must be identified and certificated by one of the examining justices. The exhibits may be retained either by the court or by the prosecution or defence, and the clerk of the court is required to notify the Crown Court, when transmitting the depositions etc, who has retained them. He sends a list of exhibits.

(h) Place of trial

The court committing an accused for trial must specify the Crown Court at which the trial is to take place, having regard to:

(i)   the convenience of the defence, the prosecution and witnesses;

(ii) the expediting of the trial;

(iii) the Lord Chancellor's directions on the distribution of Crown Court business.

(i) Committal for trial in custody or on bail

The committal of the accused to the Crown Court may be in custody, or on bail, in accordance with BA 1976 (see page 42). Where an accused has been committed in custody, he may be granted bail by the Crown Court if he is in custody for no other cause.

(j) Legal aid

Legal aid granted for the committal proceedings may be "extended" for the Crown Court proceedings; alternatively, legal aid may be granted for the Crown Court trial by the magistrates or by the Crown Court. There could be a "through" order to cover both courts (see page 104).

(k) Costs

Costs awardable in committal proceedings are dealt with at page 83-84.

(l) Committal for trial of young persons

A person under the age of 17 falling within MCA 1980 s.24(1) *(a)* or *(b)*, which prescribes the instances in which persons under that age need not be tried summarily (eg grave crimes, or jointly charged with adult), may be committed for trial on indictment by either of the methods of committal described in *(a)* or *(b)* above.

5. Summary procedure

This procedure may be for an indictable offence tried summarily, or for a simple summary offence. The form of trial before magistrates known as summary trial is based upon the form of trial on indictment. MCA 1980 s.9 and MCR 1981 rr.12–14 regulate the proceedings in magistrates' courts. Therefore, when any aspect of procedure is not provided for in the Act or the Rules, reference may be made to the procedure on indictment; magistrates have always had an inherent power to regulate procedures in their own courts in the interests of justice and a fair and expeditious trial.

(a) Where the accused appears

Guilty plea: if the accused appears, the court states the substance of the information alleging the offence, and asks the accused whether he pleads guilty or not guilty. Where counsel or solicitor appears on behalf of the accused, a plea may be entered on behalf of the accused. Where the accused pleads guilty, the court may convict him without hearing evidence.

Where the accused pleads guilty and later puts forward facts which if true would be a defence to the charge, the court will enter a plea of not guilty on his behalf. The court may allow the accused to change his plea of guilty to not guilty at any time before sentence if satisfied that justice requires it. See Table 2, page 183.

For a guilty plea to be binding and effective, it must be unequivocal and if something comes to the notice of the court which suggests the justices ought not to have accepted the guilty plea, a conviction will be upset on appeal.

Where an accused pleads guilty to an offence, but then substantially disputes some of the crucial facts which would affect sentence, the court should accept the offender's version, or hear evidence from both sides (*R* v *Williams* (1984)).

Adjournment: the court may adjourn the hearing of the information at any time before or after beginning the hearing as follows:

(i) it may fix the time and place at which the trial is to be resumed, or leave these details to be determined later by the court (or by the clerk of that court), save that if the accused is remanded the time and place must be fixed (see page 40). The court may remand the accused in custody or on bail (see page 42), but where the accused is aged 17 or over, he *must* be remanded if, in connection with the proceedings, he has previously either been in custody or remanded; otherwise the power to remand is discretionary. Note that a case is *adjourned*; an accused is *remanded*;

(ii) where the trial is adjourned, it may only be resumed if the court is satisfied that the parties have had adequate notice thereof (reasons for the adjournment should generally be included in the notice of the adjourned hearing given by the court);

(iii) after convicting the accused, the hearing may be adjourned for inquiries to be made or to determine the most suitable method of dealing with the accused. (These inquiries may be by social workers or probation officers, or medical or psychiatric experts.) However, such adjournments must not be for more than 4 weeks and if the accused is remanded in custody, the maximum is 3 weeks. The court adjourning a hearing may be composed of a single justice.

(b) Non-appearance of the accused

Where the accused fails to appear at the time and place appointed for the hearing and the prosecutor appears, the court may proceed in the accused's absence. However:

(i) the court must be satisfied that the accused had notice of the hearing a reasonable time beforehand, in accordance with MCR 1981, or that the accused has appeared on a previous occasion to answer the information;

(ii) the court cannot, in the absence of the accused, sentence him to imprisonment, detention in a detention centre, or youth custody, or order that a suspended sentence passed on him shall take effect; or impose a period of disqualification except where he has been notified after an adjournment of the court's intention to consider disqualification as a sentence or part sentence.

Issue of warrant: the court may issue a warrant under MCA 1980 s.13 for the arrest of the accused, but only in defined circumstances, and the information alleging the offence must have been substantiated on oath (for provisions as to issuing warrants in the first instance see page 12). The conditions are that:

(i) the summons previously issued has been served in accordance with MCR 1981 a reasonable time before the hearing; or the accused, being 17 or over, has appeared on a previous occasion;

(ii) the offence is punishable by imprisonment, or the court, having convicted the accused, is considering whether to disqualify the accused (usually for driving);

(iii) the power to issue a warrant under the section will only apply in relation to an adjournment of a "guilty plea by letter" hearing (see page 35) if express notice of the intention to issue a warrant has been previously given;

(iv) on adjournment, a warrant may be issued only if the court deems it undesirable by reason of the gravity of the offence to continue the trial in the absence of the accused.

Invalid proceedings where accused unaware of hearing: MCA 1980 s.14 provides that proceedings which have taken place in relation to an accused shall be avoided in certain circumstances. This applies where:

(i) the accused makes a statutory declaration that he did not know of the proceedings until a date specified in the declaration which must be after the court has begun to try the information; and

(ii) within 21 days of that date the declaration is served on the clerk to the justices.

A justice, or the justices' clerk, may accept service of the declaration after the 21 day period in (ii) above has expired, if there appears a reasonable ground for the delay. Where proceedings are avoided under this provision, the information may be tried again, but before different justices.

(c) Non-appearance of the prosecutor

If the prosecutor fails to appear at the time and place appointed for the hearing and the accused appears, the court may:

(i) dismiss the information; or

(ii) if evidence has been received on a previous occasion proceed in his absence; or

(iii) adjourn the hearing. In this case, the court may not remand the accused in custody unless he is already in custody or cannot be remanded on bail because he cannot find sureties.

(d) Non-appearance of both parties

If both the prosecutor and the accused fail to appear at the time and place of hearing, the court may dismiss the information, or if evidence has been received previously, proceed in their absence or adjourn the hearing; but where any party is represented by counsel or a solicitor he shall be deemed not to be absent.

(e) Guilty plea by letter

MCA 1980 s.12 re-enacts MCA 1957, which provides a speedy means of dealing with straightforward uncontested minor cases, where the penalty involved attracts a term of imprisonment not exceeding 3 months.

The prerequisites to the use of this procedure are that:

(i) the proceedings must be heard before a magistrates' court (not a juvenile court) and the offence is a summary offence;

(ii) the clerk of the court is notified by the prosecutor that the following documents in the prescribed form have been served with the summons upon the accused:

- a notice to the accused explaining the guilty plea procedure;
- a concise statement of the facts relating to the charge which will be placed before the court by the prosecution if the accused pleads guilty by letter; and

(iii) the clerk of the court informs the prosecutor of an indication of a guilty plea received before the hearing.

If the accused does not appear at the hearing and service of the documents mentioned above is proved, then:

(i) the court may proceed to dispose of the case in his absence and in the absence of the prosecutor, as if both parties had appeared and the accused had pleaded guilty; or

(ii) the court may decline to continue the proceedings and adjourn the hearing for the purpose of dealing with the allegation under the normal summons procedure as indicated above. In this event however, notice of the adjournment, the time and place of the adjourned hearing, and the reason therefor must be served upon the accused.

However:

(i) the accused himself may withdraw his notification of a guilty plea at any time before the hearing, whereupon the clerk must again notify the prosecutor;

(ii) the court, before convicting the accused, must have heard read out the statement of facts, the notification of the plea of guilty, and any mitigating circumstances received from the accused. The clerk of the court may read out the statement of facts. This is normally thought to be a prosecution job, but the clerk is authorised by POA 1985 Sched. 1, para. 1;

(iii) the court is prohibited from hearing any other facts of the case apart from those contained in the statement served on the accused as above;

(iv) a corporation may enter a guilty plea under these provisions but only by a director or the secretary thereof;

(v) any plea of guilty tendered must be unequivocal and be in respect of each offence if more than one is alleged;

(vi) if a possible defence to the charge is disclosed in the mitigating circumstances statement, the court must not convict the accused but adjourn the hearing for a trial. This is usually recorded as "Guilty plea not accepted, adjourn to ... for trial".

If the accused writes and pleads guilty and then turns up at court, the case can be treated as though he were not there(!) if he agrees (POA 1985 Sched. 1). However, there would probably be no prosecutor present in the court.

(f) Procedure where accused pleads not guilty

Where the accused does not plead guilty, the court must proceed in accordance with the MCR 1981. Rule 13 provides the order of evidence and speeches:

(i) the prosecutor must call evidence for the prosecution and before doing so may address the court. For an unusual case where magistrates dismissed a case after declining to hear the prosecution evidence, see *In Re Harrington* (1985). The House of Lords ordered the case re-heard, the original proceedings being a nullity.

In a magistrates' court, evidence is nearly always given by witnesses in person and on oath or affirmation. But a comparatively new innovation, CJA 1967 s.9, does provide that in criminal proceedings a written statement by any person shall be admissible as evidence as though it were oral, if some conditions are satisfied:

- the statement has to purport to be signed by the person who made it;
- the statement must contain a declaration by that person to the effect that it is true to the best of his knowledge and belief, and that he knew he would be liable to prosecution if he wilfully stated anything in it which he knew to be false or did not believe to be true;
- before the hearing, a copy of the statement must be served on the other parties;
- importantly, none of the other parties or their solicitors, within 7 days of service of the copy, must serve notice objecting to its being tendered in evidence.

The parties can, however, agree to dispense with the last two conditions.

There are other safeguards; for example if the statement is made by a person under 21, the documents shall give his age: if the statement is made by a person who cannot read, it shall be read to him before he signs and the person who read the statement shall declare that it was read: if the statement refers to any other document as an exhibit, a copy of the exhibit, not unnaturally, shall be attached to the statement, or appropriate information about inspecting the documents shall be given.

An admission can be withdrawn by leave of the court.

The starting point in all criminal trials, when there is no plea of guilty, is that the prosecution must prove its case by evidence. In general, that is not the position in civil cases, where for many years admissions about certain facts could be made by the parties. To a limited extent, formal admission of facts in criminal cases can now be made, in effect thereby not requiring the prosecution to prove facts. This is by virtue of CJA 1967 s.10 which provides that where oral evidence may be given by or on behalf of the prosecutor or defendant, then the admission by any party of such fact shall as against that party be conclusive evidence in those proceedings of the fact admitted.

It is not surprising that there are a lot of conditions before that can take place. The admission may be made before or after hearing; if it is not made in court, it shall be in writing; if it is made in writing it shall purport to be signed by the person making it (director or manager or secretary or clerk for body corporate); if made by a defendant, a person, shall be made by his counsel or solicitor; if made before trial by a person, it must be approved by his counsel or solicitor before or at the proceedings in question.

The s.10 admission is little used in practice, but can be very useful to save adjournments if a formal witness inadvertently fails to appear at court to give evidence during a trial.

If all the conditions are complied with, then in the absence of the witness, the written statement shall be read aloud at the hearing, unless only part of the statement is admitted in evidence, when an account given orally of the part not read aloud is acceptable.

(ii) evidence is given by witnesses under oath (or in the form of written statements made under CJA 1967 s.9; see also the Practice Direction at page 177); witnesses may be cross-examined;

(iii) at the conclusion of the evidence for the prosecution the accused may address the court whether or not he afterwards calls evidence. The accused should be told that he is not obliged to give evidence;

(iv) a submission that the accused has no case to answer may be made (although the court may dismiss the case of its own motion) and in this event regard should be had to the Practice Note [1962] 1 All ER 448 (see page 169). The prosecutor has a right of reply in this event. After the submission of no case to answer, a court should not allow the prosecutor to call further evidence (a second bite at the cherry) — unless for some minor evidence not seriously in dispute (R v Gainsborough Justices, ex parte Green (1983));

(v) at the conclusion of the evidence (if any) for the defence, the prosecutor may call evidence to rebut that evidence. PACEA s.79 now statutorily provides that on the trial of any person for an offence, if the defence intends to call two or more witnesses to the facts of a case, and those witnesses include the accused, then the accused shall be called before the other witness or witnesses unless the court in its discretion otherwise directs. It is not new to want the accused to give evidence before his witnesses and that is now the norm, unless the court allows otherwise. Most courts would want a good reason to allow the procedure to be otherwise than the accused first, then witnesses;

(vi) at the conclusion of the evidence for the defence and the evidence (if any) in rebuttal, the accused may address the court if he has not already done so. But note the accused shall not be entitled to make a statement without being sworn, so if he gives evidence it *must* be on oath, and liable to cross-examination. If he is not represented by counsel/solicitor he may address the court, not on oath, but only on a matter on which counsel/solicitor could have addressed the court for him (he can mitigate though, before sentence) (CJA 1982 s.72);

(vii) either party may with the leave of the court address the court a second time, but where the court grants leave to one party it shall not refuse leave to the other;

(viii) where both parties address the court twice, the prosecutor shall address the court for a second time before the accused does so;

(ix) the clerk of the court may within the discretion of the court be allowed to examine witnesses on behalf of an unrepresented party who is not competent or not desirous of doing so.

Identification evidence: Identification by recognition by witnesses can often be suspect. Wherever identity is in issue in a criminal case the court should follow the guidelines of the Court of Appeal in *R* v *Turnbull* (1976).

In brief, where a conviction depends wholly or substantially on identity evidence, the court (jury or magistrates) will be warned of the special need for caution before convicting in reliance on the correctness of identification. Identity evidence will always be scrutinized most carefully, in minute detail. The questions to be asked will include, for example, how long the witness had the accused under observation; at what distance; in what light; was the view impeded; had the witness seen the accused before; has he any special reason for remembering the accused; what was the time between the original observation and identification to police; whether there is any material discrepancy between original description and the accused's actual appearance. It is said that all those matters go to the quality of the evidence, and if the quality is good, even if there is no other evidence available, it can be sufficient to secure a conviction.

The Attorney-General issued guidelines about identity evidence in 1976, and these are reproduced at page 170. This short note is directed to evidence, rather than practice and procedure, but can be immensely important when the accused pleads not guilty.

(g) Service of summons

Service on a *person other than a corporation* may be effected by:

(i) delivering it to the person to whom it is directed; or

(ii) leaving it for him with some person at his last known or usual place of abode;

(iii) sending it by post in a letter addressed to him at his last known or usual place of abode.

However, except where registered or recorded post is used, service shall not be treated as proved in the cases of (ii) and (iii) above, unless there is some form of written acknowledgement, purporting to come from the accused or on his behalf, justifying the inference that the summons has come to the knowledge of the person to whom it is addressed.

A summons issued by a justice of the peace or justices' clerk for service on a *corporation* may be effected by delivering it at or sending it by post to the registered office of the corporation if that office is in the UK; otherwise, at or to any place in the UK where the corporation trades or conducts its business.

The service of any summons or other document required or authorised to be served may be proved by a certificate signed by the person serving the document.

(h) Remands

Where the court adjourns the hearing the accused may be remanded, ie an order of the court is made "disposing" of the person before the court on adjournment. The provisions of BA 1976 limit the court's power to remand on conditional bail or in custody.

The maximum periods of remand are as follows:

   (i) *before conviction* (MCA 1980 s.128):
- in custody: eight clear days
- on bail: eight clear days (equals 9 days) unless both parties consent to a longer period;

CJA 1982 Sched. 9 now governs a situation in which a legally represented accused, with his consent, can be further remanded in custody in his absence, but so that he will appear before the court at least every fourth remand application. The consent can be withdrawn at any time, and would result in the accused's court appearance as soon as practicable.

A custodial remand can be to another court, nearer the prison (MCA 1980 s.130).

  (ii) *after conviction or for medical reports* (MCA 1980 s.30):
- in custody: three weeks
- on bail: four weeks.

Where the accused is already serving a custodial sentence, the remand may in certain circumstances be for up to 28 days. The accused may be further remanded on bail, which may be ordered in his absence.

Where a magistrates' court remands a person in custody, after hearing full argument on an application for bail from him or his advocate, the court will issue what is called a *full argument certificate*, which will be necessary for the Crown Court before the Crown Court reviews the custody decision. Normally, in any case, there can only be one full argument for bail before a magistrates' court, thus saving repeated applications to different magistrates on the same facts, unless the second or subsequent courts are satisfied that there has been a change of circumstances or new considerations since the first custodial remand. But with the advent of an appeal, as it were, to the Crown Court against a refusal of bail, the full argument certificate was created to make sure the magistrates' court had exhausted its powers before the Crown Court became involved. The authority for this full argument certificate is CJA 1982 s.60.

Custodial remands may take the following forms:

   (i) *Police detention:* if the accused is remanded in custody, and the period is not exceeding three clear days (equals 4 days), the remand may be to detention at a police station, provided there is a need for it for inquiries into *other* offences. The detention shall cease and the accused be taken back to court as soon as the need for detention for enquiries ceases. This detention is also subject to police review procedures under PACEA 1984 s.40.

(ii) *Prison:* "commit to custody" means commit to prison; the Home Office determines the prison to which courts may commit, usually for persons over 21;

(iii) *Remand centres:* persons aged 17–20 remanded in custody are generally held in young persons' prisons and segregated from adult prisoners;

(iv) *In care:* a juvenile (under 17) not granted bail is committed not to a remand centre, but to the care of a local authority (C&YPA 1969 s.23). This is not technically a remand in custody, and the maximum period of remand after a finding of guilt is therefore four weeks.

(v) *Unruliness Certificate:* in the case of males aged over 15 years, if certain stringent conditions contained in the Certificates of Unruly Character (Conditions Order) 1977 are satisfied, the court can certify that the young person is of so unruly a character that he cannot safely be committed to care, and commit him to a remand centre or prison.

(i) Bail

Right to bail: anyone accused of an offence who appears or is brought before a magistrates' court in connection with criminal proceedings has a general right to bail, and *must* be granted bail unless his case falls within one of the exceptions in BA 1976 Sched. 1.

The general right to bail does not apply:

(i) after conviction, unless the adjournment is to obtain social enquiry or other reports (thus the general right to bail does not apply to committals to the Crown Court for sentence or to be dealt with after conviction);

(ii) to warrants to secure the appearance of the accused at court;

(iii) to offenders wishing to appeal to the Crown Court or the High Court;

(iv) to a person arrested for breach or anticipated breach of bail;

(v) to persons accused of treason.

Bail may be refused:

(i) *in all cases:*
- if the accused has been arrested for absconding or breaching bail conditions in the present proceedings;
- for the accused's own protection or welfare;
- if the accused is in custody by virtue of a sentence of a court;
- if it has not been practicable to obtain sufficient information to take a bail decision since the proceedings were instituted; or
- if the accused has been convicted and it is impracticable to complete the necessary inquiries or reports on bail;

(ii) *in the case of non-imprisonable offences only:* if the accused has previously failed to answer bail and the court believes that if released he would fail to surrender to custody;

(iii) *in the case of imprisonable offences only:* if there are substantial grounds for believing that the accused would:
- fail to surrender to custody;
- commit an offence on bail; or
- interfere with witnesses, or obstruct the course of justice.

Factors to be taken into account: the following must be taken into account by the court when considering a bail application in the case of an imprisonable offence:

(i) the nature and seriousness of the offence, and the probable method of dealing with the accused;

(ii) the accused's character and antecedents;

(iii) the accused's association and community ties;

(iv) any previous failure by the accused to comply with bail;

(v) the strength of the evidence against the accused (before conviction only);

(vi) the recent arrest of the accused and the opportunity available for enquiries;

(vii) the accused's behaviour towards and proximity to prosecution witnesses;

(viii) the behaviour and consequent likelihood of the accused's co-operation in giving information for a report;

(ix) the accused's being already subject to a custodial sentence;

(x) any other appropriate factor.

Duty to surrender: a person granted bail is under a duty to surrender to custody, usually of the court, at the end of the period of remand or at every time and place to which the hearing may be adjourned.

Requirements which the court may impose: conditions may be imposed to achieve the following objectives only:

(i) to ensure the accused surrenders to custody;

(ii) to prevent the commission of an offence while on bail;

(iii) to avoid interference with witnesses or other obstruction of justice;

(iv) to ensure the accused is available for enquiries or a report.

These objectives may be achieved by imposing any condition which the court may deem necessary, but the following are usual:

(i) provision of a surety (in imprisonable offences only), who will guarantee that the accused will surrender to custody (see below);

(ii) deposit by the accused of a security (only applicable where the accused is unlikely to remain in the UK);

(iii) a condition of residence — at home or other specified address;

(iv) a condition of regular reporting, usually at a police station, but it could be elsewhere;

(v) a condition of reporting for medical examination;

(vi) a condition that a curfew be observed.

Sureties: in considering the suitability of a surety, regard may be had, amongst other things, to the surety's:

(i) financial resources, income and capital;

(ii) character and any previous convictions;

(iii) proximity to the bailed person;

(iv) ability to prevent the accused from escaping and his willingness to do so.

The excessive imposition of sureties is forbidden by the Bill of Rights Act 1888.

Any surety may be directed to enter into the recognizance, either before the court, a justice of the peace, a justices' clerk, a police officer, inspector or above, or in charge of a police station (BA 1976 s.8(4) and (6)).

Variation of bail terms: a court may vary the conditions of bail it has granted or impose conditions where there were none before, on application by or on behalf of the bailed person or by the prosecutor or a constable.

Record of bail decisions: a record of the court's decision in imposing conditions upon an accused, and of its reasons therefor, must be kept in the court register and a copy thereof given to the accused. If the accused is remanded in custody and not legally represented the court must inform him of his right to apply to the High Court or Crown Court as the case may be for bail to be granted there.

Bail proceedings: the generally accepted procedure in dealing with remands is:

(i) an application is granted for an adjournment of the hearing;

(ii) the prosecution is then invited to make representations as to the appropriateness of bail being granted or withheld, giving reasons for so doing. Evidence of such matters is not essential but can be given;

(iii) the accused or his advocate may then make representations in the light of those made by the prosecution and put forward any matters in favour of bail; evidence may be given in appropriate cases;

(iv) the court then decides the issue; it may grant bail against the objection of the prosecutor as much as it may refuse bail in the absence of such objection. In coming to its decision it may ask for assistance, or further particulars from the parties as well as from others.

For the right of accused persons to have legal aid in bail decisions, see page 104.

6. Offences triable either way (MCA 1980 ss.17–22)

Offences triable either way consist of:

(i) those offences which are triable summarily or on indictment by virtue of statutory provisions; and

(ii) those offences listed in MCA 1980 Sched. 1.

(a) Mode of trial representations (s.1)

In any proceedings against an accused who has attained the age of 17 years relating to an either way offence the court must:

(i) ensure the charge has been written down and read to the accused; and

(ii) before hearing any evidence, hear representations first from the prosecution and then from the accused as to the mode of trial. Such representations must have regard to:

- the nature of the case;
- the circumstances which make the offence one of a serious character;
- whether the punishment which a magistrates' court would have power to inflict for the offence (if proved) would be adequate; and
- any other circumstances which appear to make it more suitable for the offence to be tried one way rather than the other. (Note that previous convictions are irrelevant in this issue and must not be made known to the court; similarly, it is thought, cases to be taken into consideration).

There is a duty on the *court* to make inquiry into the nature of the allegations.

If the prosecution is being carried out by the Attorney General or Director of Public Prosecutions, and he applies for the case to be tried on indictment the justices have no power to determine otherwise.

(b) The decision

If the court decides that trial on indictment is more appropriate it will proceed with the hearing as examining justices and committal proceedings then ensue.

If on the other hand it decides that summary trial is more appropriate, the accused must be so informed, and the court proceeds in accordance with MCA 1980 s.20 (see below).

(c) Duty to explain

Section 20 requires the court to explain to the accused in ordinary language:

(i)   that it appears to the court more suitable for the accused to be tried summarily and that he can either consent to be so tried, or if he wishes he may be tried by a jury at the Crown Court; and

(ii) that if he is tried summarily and is convicted he may be committed to the Crown Court if the convicting court, on obtaining information about his character and antecedents, previous convictions and offences taken into account, but *not* matters before the court on mode of trial representations, (eg he faces similar charges elsewhere), is of the opinion that they are such that a greater punishment should be inflicted than the convicting court has power to pass for sentence.

After explaining as above, the court must ask the accused whether he consents to be tried summarily or wishes to be tried by a jury. If he consents to be so tried, the court then proceeds to the summary trial of the information (see page 36). If he does not so consent the court proceeds to inquire into the information as examining justices (see above).

(d) Presence of the accused and other practical points

All these proceedings must take place in the presence of the accused, except:

(i)   where it is impracticable by reason of his disorderly conduct before the court. (If the accused is excluded from the proceedings for this reason and is unrepresented, and therefore unable to consent to summary trial, the court must continue proceedings as examining justices);

(ii) where the accused is absent but represented by counsel or a solicitor who in his absence signifies the accused's consent for the mode of trial proceedings to take place in his absence, and the court is satisfied there is good reason for so proceeding. If the court is not so satisfied or if for any reason the court decides to proceed as examining justices, process may issue to compel the accused's personal attendance.

The fact that the court has embarked on a summary trial, or commenced to act as examining justices does not (except for criminal damage cases, see page 48) prevent the court from changing from summary trial to inquiry at any time before the conclusion of the evidence for the prosecution, nor to change from an inquiry to summary trial; in the latter instance however, the court must explain its decision and obtain the consent of the accused to summary trial, as indicated above. See Table 1, page 181, for change of mode of trial summary. The court cannot, however, go into reverse and accept a plea of guilty, and then change to committal proceedings (*R* v *Dudley Magistrates' Court ex parte Gillard* (1984)). Evidence given during the inquiry is deemed to have been given in and for the purpose of summary trial, although witnesses may have to be recalled for cross examination.

At any time during these proceedings the court may adjourn the hearing and remand the accused. All proceedings to determine the mode of trial must take place before any evidence is called; any plea taken and conviction ordered without giving the accused the opportunity to consent to summary trial will be a nullity. The same press restrictions exist in mode of trial proceedings as they do in committal proceedings (see page 29).

The function of a magistrates' court under this procedure may be discharged by a single justice; save that where a summary trial is commenced the court must be composed of not less than two justices.

In the light of some pronouncements from the High Court, criticising the trial of "trivial" cases at the Crown Court, and the consequent higher costs involved, it can be of advantage to the accused to persuade the *justices* at the mode of trial stage to decide that the case is more suitable for trial at the Crown Court, rather than make the election for jury trial himself, thus avoiding the likelihood of having to pay high costs if convicted, because he alone chose that method of trial.

If a Crown Court trial is decided upon, there is an argument that the weaker the prosecution case, the more should the defence accept a committal for trial without consideration of the evidence. An *acquittal* can be obtained (before justices, only a *discharge* may be obtained) — leaving the possibility, however remote, of further proceedings, certainly if further evidence turns up.

(e) Offences triable either way where the value involved is small

Special rules apply to the selection of the mode of trial of most offences of criminal damage (except arson), which have the effect of denying the accused the right of Crown Court trial. These offences are contained in MCA 1980 Sched. 3, and consist solely of such offences where the value of the damage is £400 or less. As a preliminary point the court must first consider, having regard to the representations made by the prosecutor or accused, whether the value involved exceeds £400.

If the value is £400 or less the offence (which would otherwise be triable either way) must be tried summarily. If the value exceeds £400 the mode of trial procedure above applies, and representations thereon by the prosecutor and the accused follow.

If it is not clear whether the value does or does not exceed £400 the court must explain to the accused:

(i) that he can consent to be tried summarily, and that if he does so consent he will definitely be tried summarily; and

(ii) that he will not be committed to the Crown Court for greater punishment than the maximum for the lesser value offence, ie £1,000 or three months imprisonment.

The court must then ask the accused if he consents to summary trial, and if he so consents, the court proceeds as if the amount were £400 or less, but if he does not so consent, the procedure reverts back as if the value were over £400 and representations as to mode of trial then follow.

The whole "small value" procedure outlined in this section does not, however, apply where the offence charged:

(i) is one of two or more offences with which the accused is charged on the same occasion and which appear to the court to constitute a series of offences of the same or similar character. The value of the damage in this "series" exception is irrelevant (*R* v *St Helens Justices, ex parte McClorie* (1983));

(ii) consists of the incitement to commit two or more such offences.

Where the accused is jointly charged with a person who has not attained the age of 17, representations as to amount may be made by both accused.

7. General practical considerations

(a) Several offences

Where two or more offences are charged at the same time, the court should ask the accused if he consents to them being heard together; if he does not so consent the charges must be heard separately. There could be implied consent in his absence.

(b) Joinder of offenders

Several offenders may be joined in the same information, and convicted in separate penalties if the act complained of admits of the participation of several persons.

Accused who are *jointly charged* may apply to be tried separately, but in the majority of cases it is in the public interest for persons jointly charged to be tried together; even where the defence of one accused consists of an evidential attack on the other.

Where persons are *charged separately* with offences arising out of similar facts there are less compelling reasons for proceedings to be taken together; the parties should be invited to consent to the evidence being taken on the two informations at the same time, with an opportunity given to the representative of each of the parties to cross examine. Where the parties charge each other with offences, even from the same incident (cross summonses) there is no power to try them together, even if the parties consent (*R* v *Epsom Justices, ex parte Gibbons* (1984)).

The circumstances where separate trials of several accused facing similar charges was considered in *Chief Constable of Norfolk* v *Clayton* (1983). Where three accused, similarly charged with public order offences, requested separate trials, counsel for the accused and prosecutor agreeing, it was held the court was justified in ordering a joint trial, the facts being sufficiently connected (*R* v *Highbury Corner Magistrates' Court ex parte McGinley* (1986)). But there is no objection to one accused electing jury trial and being so tried, with a joint accused accepting summary trial in a relatively trivial case. It is not necessarily inimical to justice that they will be sentenced by separate courts (*In Re Gillard* (1986)).

(c) Joint charges against adults and juveniles

The legislation governing these situations is MCA s.29, and provides:

  (i) *a joint charge* involving an adult (17 +) and a juvenile (10 − 16) shall be heard by a magistrates' court that is not a juvenile court, with a power to remit the juvenile to the juvenile court for trial where the adult pleads guilty and the juvenile not guilty, or where the court proceeds as examining justices against the adult;

  (ii) a charge against a juvenile may be heard by a magistrates' court that is not a juvenile court if an adult is charged at the same time with aiding and abetting, causing or procuring, allowing or permitting the other's offence; or where the juvenile is charged with an offence arising out of circumstances which are the same as or connected with those giving rise to the offence with which the adult is charged at the same time;

(iii) a juvenile is normally tried summarily unless he is tried jointly with an adult and the court considers it necessary in the interests of justice to commit them both for trial;

(iv) an adult court finding a juvenile guilty of an offence shall remit the case to the juvenile court for sentence unless it is satisfied it would be undesirable to do so; and its powers are then usually limited to fines or discharges, anything more sophisticated being left to the juvenile court.

(See also page 15).

(d) Substitution of lesser charge

Where a prosecutor abandons a charge on which the accused appears, and proposes to proceed on a new charge, a new information should be prepared; and, if the accused desires, the case should be adjourned so he can have time to answer the charge.

(e) Change of plea and consent to summary trial

A magistrates' court may allow an accused to withdraw his plea of guilty at any time up to sentence being passed; and where he is committed to the Crown Court for sentence the Crown Court may remit the case to the magistrates for trial on the basis of a plea of not guilty. Where a plea is withdrawn, evidence of that plea is admissible at the trial. Where a plea of guilty to an either way offence is withdrawn, the justices also have a discretion to allow an accused to withdraw his consent to summary trial. See Table 2, page 183 for change of plea summary.

(f) Defect in information, summons or charge

If there is a variance between the evidence and the words of the information the prosecution is required to amend it, except where it is an insignificant detail. The power to amend is contained in MCA 1980 s.123, and permits amendment even if the information relating to summary offences is outside the normal six month time limitation.

If it appears to the court that any variance between the information and the evidence adduced on behalf of the prosecutor or complainant is such that the accused has been misled, the court, on the application of the defendant, may adjourn the hearing.

(g) Corporations

As stated earlier (page 16) corporations are generally treated in the same way as persons under the criminal law; but reference should be made to MCA 1980 Sched. 3 for detailed provisions affecting them.

In effect a corporation is committed for trial by order, and a "representative" of a corporation has rights to consent to a summary trial, and even plead guilty or not guilty at a magistrates' court trial.

(h) Delay

Inordinate delay and prejudice proved or inferred might persuade a court to prevent a case proceeding. In *R* v *Gateshead Justices, ex parte Smith* (1985), informations were laid in June 1981 for motoring offences said to have been committed in February 1981. A summons was served August 1983, but was ineffective. The case was eventually listed for hearing in July 1984, by arrest. The decision to proceed was quashed by the Divisional Court in June 1985 on the basis that it was unjust to stand trial 4 and a half years on.

(i) The justices' clerk

Throughout the maze of court practice and procedure, magistrates always have the assistance of the justices' clerk, both in court and out. The relationship between the justices' clerk and the magistrates is of crucial importance for a well run court.

The justices' clerk is not an employee, but holds an appointment, under the Justices of the Peace Act 1979. For all practical purposes, justices' clerks are appointed by some of the magistrates at his court, but no appointment is valid unless it is approved by the Home Secretary. Justices' clerks are always solicitors or barristers of five years standing, with rare exceptions.

The justices' clerk himself rarely sits in court, certainly in the larger cities, and so in a court situation, and indeed in many situations outside court, the justices are assisted by the justices' clerk's staff, who are employees, but who technically do everything in his name. The court clerks, the bread and butter of the system, who appear in court daily, comprise those who have qualified by long experience, those with a Diploma in Magisterial Law, and solicitors or barristers. Some may have law degrees, additionally.

Steps have been taken in recent years to rationalize and indeed formalize the procedure in court. The Practice Direction that controls the situation is at page 172. It was said that the first of the

Practice Directions might have curbed somewhat the overbearing clerk in court, but the present day problem is said by many to be the reluctance of the court clerk to interpose, and thus legal procedural errors occur more often than is necessary. But within the guidelines of the Practice Direction, most courts have worked out a *modus vivendi*.

(j) Contempt of court

Where any person wilfully insults the justice or justices, any witness before, or officer of, the court, or any solicitor or counsel having business in the court, during a court sitting or attendance in court, or going to or returning from the court, or wilfully interrupts the proceedings of the court or otherwise misbehaves in court, the court may order any officer of the court or any constable to take the offender into custody and detain him until the rising of the court; and the court may, if it sees fit, commit the offender to custody for a period not exceeding one month, or impose a fine or indeed both. (Contempt of Court Act 1981 s.12).

For lesser bad behaviour, such as using disrespectful or unmannerly expressions in the face of the court; using disparaging words of a judge or magistrate in relation to his office out of court; obstructing or insulting an officer of the court in the execution of his duty, but out of court, then the offender might be bound over to keep the peace, and indeed be required to find sureties for his good behaviour.

If a person persists in disrupting proceedings he will normally be ordered to leave the court provided the removal is necessary to enable the proceedings to run properly. Anyone ordered out of court who refuses might be removed by a constable or officer of the court. This is a summary, but usually most effective, way of dealing with comparatively minor disruption.

(k) Sentencing

This is not a book about sentencing, but Table 3 at page 184 might help practitioners to get quickly to "the worst" that might happen.

Chapter 5

In Court: civil proceedings

For the civil jurisdiction of the magistrates' courts and the method of commencing proceedings, see pages 3 and 18. For domestic proceedings, see Chapter 6.

1. Where the defendant appears

Where the defendant appears, the court must inform him of the substance of the complaint, and may then proceed to hear evidence or proceed otherwise as outlined below. The civil equivalent of a Not Guilty plea is "Shews Cause". The civil equivalent of a Guilty plea is "Admits", or sometimes "Consents" (to an order).

2. Adjournment

A magistrates' court may at any time, whether before or after beginning to hear a complaint, adjourn the hearing, and in doing so may fix the time and place at which the hearing is to be resumed. Unless it remands the defendant (see page 40) there is no limit on the period of adjournment. The court may leave the time and place to be determined later (or adjourn the hearing *sine die*); but the hearing shall not be resumed unless the defendant is proved to have had adequate notice thereof (see para. 8(b) below).

3. Non-appearance of the defendant

Where at the time and place appointed for the hearing or adjourned hearing of a complaint the complainant appears, but the defendant does not, the court may proceed in his absence, except that:

(a) the court shall not proceed in the absence of the defendant or issue a warrant unless either it is proved to the satisfaction of the court that the summons was served upon him within what appears to be a reasonable time before the hearing or adjourned hearing, or the defendant has appeared on a previous occasion to answer the complaint. (Rules as to service are the same as those in criminal proceedings; see page 40);

(b) if the complaint is substantiated on oath and the summons served as above, a warrant may be issued for the defendant's arrest. These are very rare.

4. Remand

Where the defendant is arrested under a warrant the court may on any subsequent adjournment of the hearing remand him; except that a warrant may not be issued, nor may the defendant be remanded, after he has given evidence in the proceedings.

On remanding the defendant the court must fix the time and place of the adjourned hearing. MCA 1980 s.128 applies to remands in civil proceedings and provides as follows:

(a) the defendant may be remanded in custody or on bail to be brought before the court at the end of the period of remand or such earlier time as the court may require; or

(b) the remand on bail shall be by taking from the defendant a recognizance (with or without sureties) — such recognizance may be taken by the court, or postponed to be taken by any person authorised, in which case the defendant is remanded in custody until the recognizance is taken.

It should be noted that remands are extremely rare in civil proceedings, and remands in custody virtually non-existent.

5. Sureties

Similar principles apply to sureties taken in connection with remands in civil matters as in criminal proceedings (see page 44).

A magistrates' court adjourning a hearing or remanding a defendant may do so composed of a single justice.

6. Non-appearance of complainant

Where at the time and place fixed for the hearing or adjourned hearing of a complaint, the defendant appears but the complainant does not, the court may dismiss the complaint, or if evidence has been received on a previous occasion, proceed in the absence of the complainant.

7. Non-appearance of both parties

Where at the time and place fixed for the hearing or adjourned hearing of a complaint, neither the complainant nor the defendant appears, the court may dismiss the complaint, but where any party is represented by counsel or a solicitor he shall be deemed not to be absent.

8. Procedure at the hearing

(a) General

MCR 1981 r.14 controls the order in which evidence may be taken in civil proceedings. It provides as follows:

- (a) the complainant calls his evidence first, but before doing so he may address the court;
- (b) at the conclusion of the complainant's evidence the defendant may address the court whether or not he afterwards calls evidence;
- (c) at the conclusion of the evidence for the defence the complainant may call evidence to rebut that evidence;
- (d) at the conclusion of the evidence for the defence, and any evidence called in rebuttal, the defendant may address the court if he has not already done so;
- (e) either party may, with the leave of the court, address the court a second time, but where the court grants leave to one party, it shall not refuse leave to the other;
- (f) where the defendant obtains leave to address the court for a second time, his second address shall be made before the second address, if any, of the complainant.

(b) Care cases

Where the father's solicitor only received the local authority reports on the morning of the hearing, and wanted to call witnesses to refute the allegations, it was contrary to natural justice to deny the father an adjournment. Early delivery of reports was essential, especially if the reports contained substantial criticisms of the parents: *K* v *K* (1986).

9. Submission of no case to answer

Once all the evidence for the complainant has been heard, the court may dismiss the case either of its own motion or on a submission. If it is a civil case the court should put the defendant to an election either to rest his case on a submission or to call evidence: *Alexander* v *Rayson* (1936) (although, where he is not put to his election he may continue and call evidence in his defence). The complainant's solicitor must be given an opportunity to address the court before it considers the issue.

In *Bond* v *Bond* (1964) it was stated there are very few matrimonial cases in which justice can be done without hearing both sides. A power to dismiss a case at the conclusion of the complainant's case should be exercised only in exceptional cases, for example where no credence can be given to the complainant's evidence or where it is crystal clear that the complainant has no case in law.

In other civil proceedings the considerations applying to criminal proceedings will apply.

10. After evidence (MCA 1980 s.53)

After hearing evidence and the parties, the court must make the order for which the complaint is made or dismiss the complaint. For example, an application by a wife to increase her children's maintenance, cannot end with an order to decrease it; it is either increased or her application is dismissed. The complainant must therefore adduce such evidence as is necessary to prove the complaint; the concept of the defendant pleading "guilty" as in criminal proceedings does not of course apply here. But the section does not require the court to hear evidence upon admitted facts (*Berkhamstead RDC* v *Duerdin-Dutton* (1964)).

11. Proceedings where no evidence is required

Where the complaint is for payment of a sum of money recoverable summarily as a civil debt, or for the variation of the rate of periodical payments, the court may make the order with the consent of the defendant without hearing any evidence.

12. Money recoverable summarily as a civil debt

MCA 1980 ss.58 and 96 provide that a magistrates' court may enforce as a civil debt payment of any sum which is ordered to be paid by a magistrates' court, except sums payable under affiliation orders or orders enforceable as such, or sums payable on summary convictions or enforceable as such.

The enforcement procedure being by complaint, is governed by MCA 1980 Parts II and III. On hearing the complaint the court may make an order for payment of the debt, which may be made by consent of the defendant without hearing evidence. Proof that it is the defendant who owes the civil debt is all that is required. Conduct and means are irrelevant at this stage; the order for payment must be served upon the debtor.

The order may require immediate payment or allow time, or payment by instalments.

Under MCA 1980 s.76, where default is made in paying a civil debt adjudged to be paid by order, a magistrates' court may issue a distress warrant, which may be executed and goods distrained under MCR 1981 r.54.

There are very limited powers in a magistrates' court to commit persons to prison or other detention in default of payment of a civil debt. MCA 1980 s.96 and MCR 1981 r.58 provide that a summons known as a "judgment summons" may be issued, but must normally be served personally, usually three clear days before the hearing. Imprisonment (maximum 6 weeks, MCA 1980 Sched. 4) may be imposed, but only where it is proved that the debtor has had the means, and refuses or neglects, or has refused or neglected, to pay.

The defendant is a compellable witness to give evidence of his means; a witness summons and warrant against him may therefore be issued.

Imprisonment imposed may be forthwith or suspended on terms.

Regard should be had to the protection against civil debt enforcement given by the Reserve and Auxiliary Forces (Protection Against Civil Interests) Act 1951.

Chapter 6

Domestic proceedings

1. Proceedings which may be brought

Proceedings under the Domestic Proceedings and Magistrates' Courts Act 1978 (see page 62); the Guardianship of Minors Acts 1971 and 1973 (see page 71); the Affiliation Proceedings Act 1957 (see page 73); and the Adoption Act 1976 (see page 75) are all domestic proceedings as defined by s.65 of the Magistrates' Courts Act 1980. There are many others but these are the bread and butter of the court dealing with domestic proceedings.

2. Commencement of proceedings

By MCA 1980 s.51 proceedings are commenced by way of complaint; if the complaint is required to be on oath it must be made to a justice of the peace; if not it may be made to the justices' clerk (see also page 18). The rules refer to complainant and defendant, but the words applicant and respondent are preferable since the DPMCA 1978 uses them. A summons will be issued to the respondent to appear at a time, date and place specified.

3. Service of summons

The summons may be served personally upon the respondent or by leaving it with some person at the respondent's last known or usual place of abode or by sending it there by post (MCR 1968 r.82). If the respondent fails to appear the court may not issue a warrant or proceed in his absence unless satisfied that the summons came to his notice (MCA 1980 s.55). Service of the summons may be proved in accordance with MCR 1981 r.99.

4. Failure of applicant to appear

If the applicant fails to appear the court may dismiss the complaint, or if evidence has been heard on a previous occasion, proceed in his/her absence.

5. Evidence

All issues of fact must be proved by evidence on oath in court; no affidavit evidence will be received. Certain orders, notably those involving a variation in the rate of periodical payments, can be made with the consent of the respondent (MCA 1980 s.53(3)). Both sides should normally be heard, and only in exceptional circumstances should cases be dismissed without hearing the respondent: *Bond* v *Bond* (1964).

(a) Order of evidence and speeches (MCR 1980 r.14) (see also page 56)

- (i) The applicant may call his evidence and before doing so he may address the court;
- (ii) the respondent may then address the court, whether or not he afterwards calls evidence;
- (iii) the applicant may call evidence in rebuttal;
- (iv) if he has not already done so the respondent may address the court;
- (v) with leave, either party may address the court for the second time. Leave must be granted to both sides if at all, and the respondent speaks first, the applicant having the last word;
- (vi) should the respondent submit there is no case to answer the applicant has the right to reply.

(b) Persons entitled to be present in court

- (i) the parties, their solicitors and counsel, witnesses and others directly concerned in the case;
- (ii) officers of the court;
- (iii) newspaper reporters (but not in adoption proceedings);
- (iv) except in adoption proceedings, any other person whom the court may permit to be present, such permission not to be withheld except on adequate grounds.

Newspaper reports may contain only those matters referred to in MCA s.71, ie the briefest details of names and addresses of the parties, the grounds of the application, a concise statement of the charges, legal points and the decision.

In practice there is nil reporting of domestic cases.

(c) Reports to the court

Under DPMCA 1978: when dealing with an application under DPMCA 1978 s.2 (see page 63), the court is *required* to consider whether there is any possibility of a reconciliation and may call for a report from a probation officer or any other person. The report must be in writing and shall state only whether any attempted reconciliation has been successful or not (DPMCA 1978 s.26).

If the application relates to child custody (see page 67), or there is a dispute between two persons having parental rights or duties (see page 68), the court may call for reports from an officer of the local authority or a probation officer (DPMCA 1978 s.12(3)). The report shall be made to the court hearing the application and, if it is in writing, a copy must be given to each party. The person making the report may be required to give evidence.

Under GA 1973: by GA 1973 s.6, similar reports may be obtained where application is made under GMA 1971 s.9 (see page 71).

As to means: By MCA 1980 s.27, the court may request a probation officer to report on the means of the parties when a money payment order is likely to be made or enforced. No such report can be called for until all the substantive issues have been decided. By MCA 1980 s.100, a statement in writing signed by an employer shall be evidence of wages received.

Blood Tests (Family Law Reform Act 1969 s.20): Where paternity is in dispute (see page 75) any party to the proceedings may request the court to give directions for the use of blood tests to assist in determining the issue. For procedure see Home Office Circulars 248/1971, 55/1979 and 23/1980; also the Magistrates' Court (Blood Test) Rules 1971. The person applying has to pay the justices' clerk the fees for the sampler and tester, normally within 14 days. Photographs of the subjects are also normally required.

6. Refusal of orders in cases more suitable for the High Court

If the magistrates' court is of the opinion that the case may more conveniently by dealt with in the High Court, it shall refuse to make an order: no appeal lies from such a refusal (DPMCA 1978 s.27; GMA 1971 s.16; CA 1975 s.111). Problems with polygamous marriages might be suitable.

7. Proceedings under the Domestic Proceedings and Magistrates' Courts Act 1978

(a) Jurisdiction

Application for an order under DPMCA 1978 is to made at the court for the area in which either the applicant or the respondent resides. Application can be made if the respondent resides in Scotland or Northern Ireland, if the applicant resides in England or Wales and the parties last resided as man and wife in England or Wales; or if the applicant resides in Scotland or Northern Ireland and the respondent resides in England or Wales (s.30).

"Resides" denotes some degree of permanence: *Macrae* v *Macrae* (1949).

Either party to the marriage may make application for an order. There are court orders in existence for wives to pay maintenance to their husbands.

References below are to the DPMCA 1978 unless otherwise stated.

(b) Orders for payment of money

Orders for payment of money, periodical payments and "lump sum", may be made on the grounds that the respondent has:

    (i) failed to provide reasonable maintenance for the applicant; or

   (ii) failed to provide or to make proper contribution towards reasonable maintenance for any child of the family.

       The "failure to provide" need not be wilful; mere neglect is sufficient. A "child of the family" is a child of both parties, or a child who had been treated by both of the parties as a child of the family (other than a child boarded out by a local authority or voluntary organisation) (s.88); or

  (iii) behaved in such a way that the applicant cannot reasonably be expected to live with the respondent.

       "Reasonably" qualifies "expected to live with" and not "behaviour". It is for the court to decide in each case what is "reasonable"; the test is "would any right thinking person come to the conclusion that this respondent has behaved in such a way that this applicant cannot reasonably be expected to live with him taking into account the whole of the circumstances and the characters and personalities of the parties" (*Livingstone-Stallard* v *Livingstone-Stallard* (1974)).

A complaint under this heading must normally be made within 6 months of the conduct complained of.

There is no automatic right to an order because of a party's adultery; adultery by the applicant is now no absolute bar to an order; or

(iv) has deserted the applicant.

Desertion requires a factual separation, an intention to desert, an absence of consent by the deserted party, and that there should be no just cause for the separation. The parties must be living as two separate households. The intention to desert must be proved and must amount to an intention by the deserting spouse to bring the marriage to an end. If the parties agree to separate there is no desertion and if the respondent was justified in leaving, eg by the conduct of the applicant, he is not in desertion.

(s.1)

See page 149 for a form of complaint.

The court may make one or more of the following orders under s.2, if one of the above grounds is proved:

(i) that the respondent make to the applicant such periodical payments and for such term as may be specified in the order;

(ii) that the respondent pay to the applicant such lump sum not exceeding £500 as may be so specified;

(iii) that the respondent make to the applicant for the benefit of the child of the family to whom the application relates, or *to* such child, such periodical payments, and for such term, as may be specified;

(iv) that the respondent pay to the applicant for the benefit of the child of the family to whom the application relates, or *to* such child, such lump sum, not exceeding £500, as may be so specified.

By s.11, if the court is not satisfied that there are grounds for making an order in favour of the applicant, but exercises its powers to give custody of a child to one of the parties, orders under (iii) and (iv) above can be made. Where custody is given to a parent who is not a party to the marriage, orders for periodical payments can nevertheless be made against a party to the marriage. If the child is committed to the care of a local authority under s.10 (see page 68), an order for periodical payments can be made against a party to the marriage.

Payments may be ordered from the date of the application or from the date of the hearing; similarly they may run from some date in the future, eg a date by which it is anticipated that the person liable to make payments will have found a job. Payments need not be weekly and may be for a limited period.

Consideration should be given to the tax position of the applicant; there may be a saving of income tax if payments for a child were to be made direct to the child. Payments other than for children's maintenance cease on the remarriage of the person in whose favour they were made, or upon the death of either party.

Small maintenance payments: Weekly payments *to* a wife/husband below £48 (£208 monthly), *to* a child below £48 (£208 monthly), or *for* a child below £25 (£108 monthly) are "small maintenance payments". The figures are correct at April 1986. This means the money is paid across as ordered, without deduction of tax at source — an important factor for (normally) an impoverished wife.

Payments are always to be made through the court unless specifically ordered otherwise.

There may be more than one lump sum, and if ordered at different times, the aggregate may exceed £500.

When making an order for the payment of money the court must consider (s.3, and The Matrimonial and Family Proceedings Act 1984), first, the welfare while a minor of any child of the family under 18 and then:

    (i)   the income, earning capacity, property and other financial resources which each of the parties to the marriage has or is likely to have in the foreseeable future, including in the case of earning capacity any increase in that capacity which it would in the opinion of the court be reasonable to expect a party to the marriage to take steps to acquire;

    (ii) the financial needs, obligations and responsibilities which each of the parties to the marriage has or is likely to have in the foreseeable future;

    (iii) the standard of living enjoyed by the parties to the marriage before the occurrence of the conduct which is alleged as the ground of the application;

(iv) the age of each party to the marriage and the duration of the marriage;

(v) any physical or mental disability of either parties to the marriage;

(vi) the contributions which each of the parties has made or is likely in the foreseeable future to make to the welfare of the family, including any contribution by looking after the home or caring for the family;

(vii) the conduct of each of the parties, if that conduct is such that it would in the opinion of the court be inequitable to disregard it.

For child maintenance or lump sum:

(i) the financial needs of the child;

(ii) the income, earning capacity (if any), property and other financial resources of the child;

(iii) any physical or mental disability of the child:

(iv) the standard of living enjoyed by the family before the occurrence of the conduct which is alleged as the ground of the application;

(v) the manner in which the child was being and in which the parties to the marriage expected him to be educated or trained;

(vi) the matters mentioned in relation to the parties to the marriage in paragraphs (i) and (ii) first above.

Where maintenance is to be in favour of a child of the family who is not a child of the respondent, the court shall also have regard to:

(i) whether the respondent had assumed any responsibility for the child's maintenance and, if he did, the extent to which, and the basis on which, he assumed that responsibility and the length of time during which, he discharged that responsibility;

(ii) whether in assuming and discharging that responsibility the respondent did so knowing that the child was not his own child;

(iii) the liability of any other person to maintain the child.

Similarly, the financial needs and resources of each child must be considered.

"Earning capacity" includes the availability of work and the ability to earn higher wages: *McEwan* v *McEwan* (1972): *Klucinski* v *Klucinski* (1953).

"Property" includes the value of assets dissipated but not the profit from a business run by the respondent and his mistress: *Lombardi* v *Lombardi* (1973); neither must the income of a mistress or a second wife be taken into account: *Macey* v *Macey* (1981). However, the existence of a mistress or second wife is relevant if the respondent is under a duty to support her. Where the marriage is of short duration, the payments may be reduced, especially if there are no children: *Graves* v *Graves* (1973). Note that maintenance payments should not push the payer below subsistence level, possibly the amount he would receive on supplementary benefit.

Age limits on orders in respect of children (s.5): in the first instance no order may extend beyond the birthday of the child next following his attaining the upper limit of compulsory school age (ie 17). No order shall be made in favour of a child who has attained the age of 18 years unless:

(i) he is or will be receiving instruction at an educational establishment or undergoing training for a trade, profession or vocation; or

(ii) there are some other special circumstances.

Consent orders (s.6): where the amount of any periodical payment (and any lump sum) has been agreed between the parties, but the applicant feels she needs some security in addition to the respondent's promise to pay, an order may be made under this section. No order may be made in respect of a child unless it provides for, or makes a proper contribution towards, the financial needs of the child. The court will normally make the order where satisfied the respondent has agreed, and has no reason to think that it would be contrary to the interests of justice to exercise those powers.

It is becoming almost universal for a s.2 application to be turned into a s.6 agreed order, whereupon the s.2 application is treated as withdrawn.

Forms of complaint and consent are set out at page 150.

Orders where there is consensual separation (s.7): if the parties have lived apart for at least 3 months and there are no grounds for an order under s.1, the applicant may obtain an order where voluntary payments have been made but where there is no agreement as to amount.

The aggregate of payments within the 3 months after making the order may not exceed the aggregate of payments during the preceding 3 months, nor may they exceed the amount the court would have ordered had the application been made under s.1.

See page 152 for a form of complaint under s.7.

Interim orders (s.19): the court has power to make interim orders for payments and custody at any time before the final determination of the application.

Variation etc of orders (ss.20–24): there is a wide discretion to vary, revive or revoke orders for periodical payments and to order lump sum payments; and to vary or revoke custody orders.

Enforcement of orders (s.32): orders for the payment of money are to be enforced as if they were affiliation orders (see page 79).

Maintenance Orders Act 1958: This statute makes a comprehensive provision for enabling maintenance orders to be registered:

(i) in the case of an order made by the High Court or a county court, in the magistrates' court; and

(ii) in the case of an order made by a magistrates' court, in the High Court.

Once registered, those orders can be enforced in like manner as an order made by the court of registration, and in the case of an order registered in a magistrates' court, can be varied by a magistrates' court. But note that orders made under Part III, MFPA 1984 in the High Court (overseas divorce etc) can only be *enforced* if registered in a magistrates' court, not *varied*.

This is mostly a one way traffic with High Court and divorce court orders being registered in a magistrates' court, really because of the easier enforcement. It means that all payments go through the magistrates' court office, as opposed to being paid direct, and the simplicity of issuing summonses for non-payment encourages registration.

(c) Orders for the custody of and access to children (s.8)

The court may not make or refuse to make an order for financial provision until it has decided all questions relating to the custody of and access to any child of the family. The welfare of the child is the first and paramount consideration (s.15).

Custody may not be given to a person who is neither a parent nor a party to the marriage (but see CA 1975 s.33, page 78). Custody may not be given to more than one person. An order for custody is of no effect when the child attains the age of 18 years. For a "stay" of custody order, see subs.(6). A court can direct, eg, that there be no change of custody by virtue of its order until an appeal has been heard; in other words, a stay until the occurrence of an event, or for a period of time, as specified. The order could, for example, be stayed for 7 days, on a change of custody, to allow a "civilised" changeover of school, clothing and toys, the move and so on. No order for custody may be made where the child is in the care of a local authority or there is already a custody order of another court in force.

By s.9, in exceptional circumstances, an order may be made that the child shall be under the supervision of a local authority or a probation officer; and by s.10, a child under 17 years may be committed to the care of a local authority if the court is satisfied it is undesirable or impractical for custody to be entrusted to either of the parents.

By s.34, a clause may be inserted in the order that the child shall not be taken out of England and Wales without the leave of the court.

When exercising its powers under s.8, the court may make an order on the application of a grandparent that access to the child should be given to that grandparent. By GMA 1971 s.14A, a grandparent may apply for access to a minor in certain circumstances (eg where a custody order is in force or application for such an order has been made).

Where persons have parental rights or duties as a result of an order under s.8 and there is a dispute, the court may be asked to give directions on that specific issue.

See pages 153 and 154 for forms of notice of the court's powers to make provision in respect of children, to be given to the parties to the case.

(d) Effect of continued co-habitation

By s.25, orders for payments under ss.2, 6, 11 and 19, and orders for custody, remain enforceable if the parties continue to live together or resume co-habitation, but cease to have effect if the co-habitation exeeds a continuous period of 6 months. This 6 month rule does not apply if the order is for payments to be made direct to a child; if it gives custody to a parent who is not a party to the marriage; or if it applies ss.9 or 10 (see above). An order under s.7 (see page 66) ceases to have effect immediately the parties resume living together.

(e) Appeals (s.29)

Appeal from a magistrates' court's decision to make an order or to vary or revoke an order, or the refusal to do so, lies to the High Court. There is no power to state a case on a point of law under DPMCA 1978. See further page 120 *et seq.*

(f) Reciprocal Maintenance Enforcement

The Maintenance Orders (Facilities for Enforcement) Act 1920 and the Maintenance Orders (Reciprocal Enforcement) Act 1972 provide for the enforcement of maintenance orders made in England and Ireland and in Her Majesty's Dominions outside the UK, and then further for the transmission of maintenance orders made in the UK for enforcement in a reciprocating country.

One way or another, an existing maintenance order made in the UK can be enforced in many countries thousands of miles away. The list does vary from time to time, and the practical situation is that the local justices' clerk should be approached to see whether or not the order might be enforceable in any particular country, Commonwealth or otherwise. Similarly, orders made in certain foreign countries might well be enforced in a magistrates' court in the UK.

The procedure both ways is often complex, and a refinement is that a *provisional* maintenance order might be made in this country, for confirmation or otherwise by the courts of foreign countries. The case there proceeds on the basis of depositions taken here, which can be questioned in an overseas court. No-one entering the realms of cross world maintenance enforcement should think that the procedure is quick and easy; far from it.

UK orders are usually channelled through the Home Office, Foreign Office and then to the foreign courts, but with determination orders can be so enforced. Most documents leaving the UK for foreign climes for enforcement would need photographs of the person who is supposed to be paying to avoid getting the wrong man.

(g) Personal protection orders and exclusion orders (s.16)

Either party to a marriage may make an application to the court for an order that the respondent shall not use or threaten to use violence against the person of the applicant and/or a child of the family. The court has to be satisfied that the respondent has used violence or threatened violence against the applicant or a child of the family, and that the order is necessary for the protection of the applicant and/or the child (s.16(2)). This is a Personal Protection Order. See page 155 for a form of complaint.

If the court is satisfied that the respondent has used or threatened violence against the applicant or a child of the family *and* has used violence upon some other person, or is in breach of an order under s.16(2), and that the applicant or child is thus in physical danger, or would be in danger if they entered the matrimonial home, the court may make an Exclusion Order. This requires the respondent to leave the matrimonial home, and/or prohibits him from entering it, and further requires him to permit the applicant to enter and remain there (s.16(3) and (4)).

An order under s.16(2) and (3) may be subject to conditions and exceptions and may last for a specified time.

The hearing should be before a domestic court but if there is some urgency any properly constituted magistrates' court will do; there are restrictions on who may be present and on newspaper reports.

Procedure: The summons must be served personally together with a notice (see page 155) explaining the court's powers. However, if one justice is satisfied by evidence on oath that personal service is impractical then service may be by post or by leaving it with some person at the respondent's last known or usual place of abode.

An application under s.16(3) must be heard as soon as possible and in any event not later than 14 days after the issue of the summons.

A copy of the court's order must be served personally or by post, and no warrant of commitment for a breach can be issued until the order has been served, unless the respondent was present and the warrant was issued at that time.

Expedited orders (s.16(6)): if the applicant for an order under s.16(2) (but not s.16(3) or (4)) satisfies the court in writing that there is imminent danger to herself or a child of the family, an order can be made under s.16(2), notwithstanding that no summons has been served on the respondent or that he has been summoned for a different time or place. The matter must be heard as soon as practicable and may be before a single justice.

An expedited order takes effect either on the date on which it is served or upon some later specified date, and ceases to have effect 28 days after it is made or on the commencement of the hearing for the full order, whichever is first.

By s.17, orders made under s.16 can be varied or revoked and further orders can be made.

Powers of arrest (s.18): if an order is made that the respondent shall not use violence against the applicant or a child of the family, or shall not enter the matrimonial home (s.16(2)), and the court is satisfied that he has injured the applicant or child in the past and is likely to do so again, a power of arrest may be attached to the order. A constable may then arrest the respondent if he acts in breach of the order and take him before a justice within 24 hours; in urgent cases it is not necessary for this hearing to take place in a court house.

The respondent may be remanded on bail or in custody and eventually punished for the breach in accordance with MCA 1980 s.63(3).

If an order without a power of arrest is contravened the applicant may apply to a justice to issue a warrant; the information must be substantiated on oath (see page 156 for a form of application). Alternatively, s.63(3) may be used.

8. Guardianship of minors

Application for custody of a minor may be made under GMA 1971 s.9 as amended by GA 1973, where it is inappropriate to apply for an order under DPMCA 1978 s.8 (see page 67).

(a) Jurisdiction (GMA 1971 s.15)

Application may be made at the magistrates' court for the area in which the applicant, the respondent or the minor resides. Section 15(3), (4) and (6) applies where one of the parents resides in Scotland or Northern Ireland.

(b) Who may apply

Either parent wishing to obtain custody and/or access to his child, including his adopted child, may make an application by complaint (for a form, see page 157). The child must be under 18 years of age at the date of the hearing. The parent of an illegitimate child may apply but there can be no order for maintenance under this Act, only under APA 1957.

In certain circumstances grandparents may apply for access (GMA 1971 s.14A).

(c) Powers of the court

The welfare of the infant is the first and paramount consideration, always, in deciding what, if any, order the court should make (GMA 1971 s.1).

The court may order legal custody to either parent; in addition there is usually an order for access to the parent excluded from custody.

Legal custody may not be awarded to more than one person (GMA 1971 s.11A). The parent excluded from custody may be ordered:

(i) to make such periodical payments for the benefit of the minor and/or

(ii) to pay a lump sum, not exceeding £500, for the benefit of the minor

as the court thinks fit.

Such payments may be ordered to the other parent or to the minor. See page 64 for the tax position on small maintenance payments.

A clause may be added that the minor shall not be taken from England or Wales without leave of the court (GMA 1971 s.13A).

In exceptional circumstances, an order may be made that the minor shall be under the supervision of a local authority or probation officer (GA 1973 s.2(2)(a)); and by s.2(2)(b) he may be committed to the care of the local authority if the court is satisfied that it is impractical or undesirable for custody to be granted to either parent.

(d) Age limits (GMA 1971 s.12)

In the first instance no order for payments may extend beyond the birthday of the minor next following his attaining the upper limit of compulsory school age, ie 17. No order may extend beyond the minor's 18th birthday unless:

(i) he is or will be receiving instruction at an educational establishment or undergoing training for a trade, profession or vocation whether or not he also has a job; or

(ii) there are some other special circumstances.

(e) Matters to be taken into consideration (GMA 1971 s.12A)

The court must take account of the following matters before making a money payment order:

(i) the income and other resources of the parents;

(ii) their financial needs and obligations;

(iii) the financial resources and the needs of the minor;

(iv) any physical or mental disability of the minor.

(f) Variation of orders (GMA 1971 ss.9, 12B and 12C)

There is a wide discretion to vary, suspend or revive these orders, and to order lump sum payments.

Where the minor has attained the age of 16 years, he may apply for a variation in the rate of periodical payments. If the order ceases at any time before the minor attains 18 years, then at any time before he is 21 he may apply for the order to be revived.

(g) Interim orders (GA 1973 s.2(4))

If the application is adjourned, an interim order may be made in respect of periodical payments and in special circumstances, as to custody and access. No interim order, or the aggregate period of such orders if there is more than one, may exceed six months (DPMCA s.19(6)). Further, no interim order for access can be made in favour of the father of an illegitimate child, until his paternity is proved (*Re O (a Minor)*(1985)).

(h) Effect of continued co-habitation (GA 1973 s.5A)

Orders for custody and maintenance remain enforceable if the parents continue to live together or resume co-habitation, but cease to have effect if the co-habitation exceeds a continuous period of 6 months. This 6 month rule does not apply where payments are made direct to the minor, or where there is a supervision order.

(i) Appeals

Appeals lie to the Family Division of the High Court; see page 120.

9. Affiliation

(a) Jurisdiction

Application under the Affiliation Proceedings Act 1957 should be made to the magistrates' court for the area where the mother resides; temporary residence will suffice if she has no permanent residence.

(b) Who may apply

(i) a single woman who is pregnant with a child that will be born illegitimate, or whose illegitimate child has been born. "Single woman" means single at the date of birth; and includes a married woman who can prove non-access at the material time by her husband;

(ii) where accommodation or assistance is provided for an

illegitimate child, the Supplementary Benefits Commission or a local authority;

(iii) the custodian of a child under CA 1975 s.45 where he is not married to the mother, provided application is made within 3 years of the custodianship order.

(c) Time limits

Complaints must be made:

(i) before birth (in which case the mother must make the complaint upon oath);

(ii) at any time within three years of the birth;

(iii) at any time upon proof that the alleged father has paid money for the maintenance of the child within three years of its birth. Money paid for a gift of clothing for the child is enough;

(iv) within 12 months of the alleged father's return to the UK upon proof that he ceased to reside in England within three years of the birth.

See pages 157 and 158 for forms of complaint.

(d) Powers of the court (s.4)

The court may make the following orders:

(i) that the defendant is the putative father;

(ii) that he make periodical payments to or for the maintenance of the child (see page 64 for the small maintenance payments tax position);

(iii) that he make a lump sum payment not exceeding £500.

Section 5(4) provides for the situation where the mother is of unsound mind.

The income and other financial resources and the needs and obligations of the mother, the putative father and the child have to be taken into account.

(e) Persons entitled to payments

The mother, the child or the local authority having the child in its care may receive payments under an affiliation order.

(f) Age limits (s.6)

No order may be made if the child is 18 years of age.

Payments may run from the date of making the application or any later date, and in the first instance cease on the date of the child's birthday following his attaining school leaving age.

Payments may be ordered to continue after the child attains 18 years if he is receiving instruction at an educational establishment or training for a trade, profession or vocation, whether or not he also has a job.

By s.7, no payments may continue after the child has attained 16 years if he is in care, unless he is living with his mother; and no such payments may be ordered to anyone other than the child himself or his mother or the person having legal custody of him. Maintenance payments may be back-dated to the birth of the child provided the complaint was made within two months of the birth.

(g) Evidence

If paternity is admitted the mother does not have to give evidence. In a case where she does give evidence (usually where paternity is denied) there must be some corroboration, ie some other evidence of the probability that the defendant is the father.

The defendant is a competent witness for the complainant (and is compellable if summoned as a witness; a warrant may be issued if he fails to answer a witness summons).

(h) Blood tests

See page 61.

(i) Appeals

Appeals lie to the Crown Court; see page 114.

10. Adoption

The Adoption Act 1976 will, when it comes into force, repeal but re-enact and improve the Adoption Act 1958. Meantime, the Act of 1958 controls, but the Children Act 1975 amends it considerably.

(a) Effect of adoption order

An adoption order vests parental rights and duties in the adopters.

The order extinguishes the rights and duties vested in any other person, including the duty to maintain the child (but not where an agreement constitutes a trust, or provides the duty is not to be extinguished).

(b) The application

The Magistrates' Courts (Adoption) Rules 1984 specify the form to be used; these rules also detail the procedure to be followed. See form of application for adoption at page 162. All applications are to the domestic court. The hearing is "in camera".

(c) Who may apply

Application may be made jointly by a married couple provided each has attained the age of 21 years and at least one of them is domiciled in the UK, the Channel Islands or the Isle of Man.

No joint application may be made unless the applicants are married to each other.

Application may be made by one person provided he has attained the age of 21 years and is domiciled as above; a married person applying alone must satisfy the court that his spouse cannot be found or is incapable through ill-health of making an application, or that they are permanently separated.

The parent of a child applying alone must satisfy the court that the other parent is dead or cannot be found or that there are some other special circumstances justifying his exclusion from notice of the application.

When dealing with an application, the court must have regard to the possibility of custodianship (see below), an alternative to adoption, certainly where an applicant is a step-parent.

(d) Who may be adopted

Application may be made in respect of any unmarried child under the age of 18 years.

Where one of the applicants is a parent, step-parent or relative of the child, or if the child was placed by an adoption agency, an order cannot be made unless the child is at least 19 weeks old and, during the 13 weeks preceding the application, had his home with the applicant.

In all other cases no order can be made unless the child is at least 12 months old and has had his home with the applicant for 12 months.

(e) Parental agreement

No order can be made without the unconditional agreement of the child's actual parents or legal guardian. The agreement of the father of an illegitimate child is not required unless he is the legal guardian. Agreement may be dispensed with by court order, when the parent or guardian:

(i)   cannot be found or is incapable of giving agreement;

(ii) is withholding agreement unreasonably;

(iii) has persistently failed, without reasonable cause, to discharge his parental duties;

(iv) has abandoned or neglected the child;

(v)   has persistently ill-treated the child;

(vi) has seriously ill-treated the child — if the rehabilitation of the child in the household is unlikely.

Parental agreement is not necessary if the child has been "freed for adoption" — this is a court order, which pre-empts the parental agreement necessary, when adoption proceedings may not be imminent, but contemplated for the future. A "Free for adoption" order can be revoked.

The agreement of the mother is ineffective if given less than 6 weeks after the birth.

(f) Adoption applications

Adoption applications fall into two categories:

(i)   "open", where the parties know who the others are;

(ii) "confidential" where the applicants want their identity kept from other parties, usually the father/mother. Here the applicants notify the justices' clerk and he allocates a serial number. The other parties then know only the serial number of the case.

But eventually, all adopted children can ascertain their true parents, after compulsory counselling.

(g) Appeals

Appeals lie to the High Court, Family Division; see page 120.

11. Custodianship

The custodianship provisions became effective on 1 December 1985.

Section 33, CA 1975 is applicable where a person who is not a parent of a child wishes to obtain legal custody. In proceedings under GMA 1971 and DPMCA 1978 there is no power for a person who is neither a parent nor a party to the marriage in question to apply for custody. If the court wishes to give custody to such a person, he may be treated as if he had made an application for a custodianship order (CA 1975 s.33). See page 158 for the form of application.

There is a similar power in adoption proceedings and custodianship *must* be considered where an applicant is a step-parent.

(a) Jurisdiction

The child must be in England or Wales (s.33) and the application must be made to the court in whose area he is (CA 1975 s.100). However, proceedings may be brought by or against a person who is outside England and Wales (CA 1975 s.46).

A summons is not necessary unless there is an application for maintenance; notice of the application must be given to the local authority (CA 1975 s.40).

(b) Who may apply

    (i) a relative or step-parent provided he has the consent of the person with legal custody, and the child has had his home with the applicant for the 3 months preceding the application;

    (ii) any other person provided he has the consent of the person with legal custody and the child has had his home with the applicant for at least 12 months including the 3 months preceding the application;

    (iii) any other person with whom the child has had his home for 3 years including the 3 months preceding the application.

There are circumstances in which no-one has legal custody of a child, and then a custodianship case can start without any consent.

The parent of the child is not qualified to make an application. As a general rule, a step-parent is not qualified to apply if an order for custody was made in divorce or nullity proceedings.

(c) Powers of the court

    (i) A custodianship order; the order vests legal custody of a child in a person other than one of its parents. It is appropriate, for example, where a child has for a long time been brought up by relatives or foster parents who normally have no legal status with regard to the child;

(ii) to order that the parents or grandparents may have access to the child (provided they make application);

(iii) to revoke or vary any existing order for maintenance;

(iv) to make orders for lump sum and periodical payments by parents to the custodian as if the matter were an application under DPMCA 1978 (see page 62).

(v) to make supervision and care orders where appropriate (see page 67).

Note that a local authority can make contributions to a custodian towards the cost of the accommodation and maintenance of the child. It is thought that many custodianship applications could be local authority inspired.

By s.43A(1) a clause may be added that the child shall not be taken from England and Wales without leave of the court.

(d) Variation etc of orders

Section 35 provides for the variation and revocation of custodianship orders. Applicants and respondents will be the custodian, the parents *and* the local authority.

(e) Interim orders

Section 34(5) provides that interim orders may be made as if the matter were a guardianship application (see page 73).

(f) Appeals

Appeals lie to the High Court, Family Division; see page 120.

12. Enforcement of money orders in domestic proceedings (MCA 1980 s.93)

(a) Failure to pay

If the person ordered to make payments fails to do so, he may be summoned before the court for an inquiry into his means. The complaint may be made by the person entitled or by the justices' clerk on (usually) her behalf. No arrears may be enforced until

15 days after the order is made. The means inquiry is usually held at the court for the area in which the non-payer resides.

(b) Powers of the court

Attachment of earnings order: this order is directed to the non-payer's employer and orders him to deduct each week a fixed amount from the non-payer's wages and send it to the court. This "normal deduction rate" is fixed by the court and should be enough to meet the weekly payments plus an additional amount to reduce the arrears. The court must also fix a "protected earnings rate", earnings below which no deductions can be taken by the employer.

Once the arrears have been paid, the normal deduction rate will be reduced to the amount of the weekly payments required by the original order, or be discharged. An attachment order is only effective if the defaulter has steady employment.

Imprisonment: a regular defaulter may be committed to prison for a period not exceeding 6 weeks. The court must be satisfied that the default is due to his wilful refusal or culpable neglect to pay and that an attachment of earnings order is inappropriate (MCA 1980 s.93(6)).

The committal may be suspended on terms that the defaulter pays a regular sum to the court (MCA 1980 s.77).

Section 18, Maintenance Orders Act 1958 provides the procedure to be adopted should the default continue. The defaulter is to be sent a notice stating that the commitment warrant falls to be issued, and gives the defaulter 7 days to notify the reason for default. A justice can refer that reason to a court, for further consideration, with a view to further suspension, or order the commitment warrant to issue forthwith.

There is no obligation on the court to inform the defaulter of possible legal aid before committing to prison (*R* v *Cardiff Justices ex parte Salter* (1985)).

Note that a court can remit arrears accrued, on enforcement or variation proceedings, but would be looking for good reason. Magistrates' courts follow divorce court guidelines that it may not be appropriate to enforce arrears over one year old. Before remission of arrears, the person owed the money should be consulted by the court (*R* v *Camberwell Green Justices ex parte Pattison and Dickens* (1985)).

(c) Appeals

An appeal relating to the enforcement of an order would appear to be dealt with by way of case stated (RSC 1965 O.56 and MCA 1980 s.111).

Chapter 7

Costs

1. Criminal jurisdiction

Please note that the provisions set out below will be modified when the Crown Prosecution Service (see page 7) comes fully into operation late in 1986. The Costs in Criminal Cases Act 1973 will be repealed and replaced. A note appears on page 87 about the new provisions.

(a) Introduction: Costs in Criminal Cases Act 1973

The powers of magistrates' courts to award costs in criminal proceedings are contained in CCCA 1973. The court may order costs in two ways:

(i) that the costs of one side be borne by the other (*inter partes*);

(ii) that the costs of one side or the other or both be borne by central government funds, in indictable offence cases.

Sometimes both types of order may be made in the same case.

Exercise of the courts' powers depends partially upon the nature of the proceedings (summary or committal), and the nature of the offence charged (summary or indictable).

Any party to proceedings who makes an application for costs under any of these headings should be able to give precise details of his claim to the court at the hearing, especially in summary cases where costs can only be *inter partes*. In other (indictable) cases it is common practice, once the costs order is made, for the justices' clerk to fix the costs ordered from central funds in chambers, out of court.

(b) Summary trial of summary offences

On dismissing the information, the court may make such order for

81

costs to be paid by the prosecutor to the accused as it thinks just and reasonable. The order could be on a date after withdrawal of proceedings.

On convicting the accused, the court may make such order for costs to be paid by the offender to the prosecutor as it thinks just and reasonable (but costs of less than 25p, save in exceptional circumstances, cannot be ordered; and, in the case of a juvenile, costs shall not exceed the amount of any fine). The costs may include an amount in respect of an investigating officer (not a police officer) paid out of public funds, whose job it was to investigate alleged offences (*Neville* v *Gardner Merchant Ltd* (1984)). But there are limits. The Divisional Court will quash a harsh and oppressive costs order, eg an unreasonably high figure for many charges arising from the same circumstances (*R* v *Tottenham Justices, ex parte Joshi* (1982)).

In both the above instances, if the court makes an order it must specify the amount of costs there and then. Having said that, in an exceptionally difficult case, the question of costs could be adjourned for full argument when the claims were fully set out later. Summary costs may not be left to the justices' clerk to ascertain, but he can enquire about and advise on them: *Bunston* v *Rawlings* (1982).

Court's discretion to award: in fixing the amount, indeed the award itself, the court may take into account a number of factors (eg whether the prosecution should have been brought; whether prosecution or defence has behaved badly), but the award should not breach the principle that an award is intended only as an indemnity.

Court's duty to have regard to means: both parties are entitled to address the court as to means. The court should have some information upon which to base its award, which should be arrived at with regard to the payer's means.

Prosecution's claim: all the prosecution costs which are incurred in or about the prosecution and conviction of the offender may be claimed, including lawyer's fees, loss of earnings of witnesses, (but not loss of time by the prosecutor in preparation and presentation: *R* v *Stockport Magistrates' Court, ex parte Cooper* (1984)), expenses, doctor's expenses in visiting and examining the defendant; provided all are considered by the court to be just and reasonable. Costs may be claimed by the prosecutor in cases dealt with by guilty plea by letter under MCA 1980 s.12 (see page 35), but some courts will not grant).

Enforcement of payment of costs: Costs payable by the offender are enforceable in accordance with AJA 1970 s.41(1) and Sched. 9, Part I. Any sum payable under an order for costs is treated as if it had been imposed as a fine on conviction, and is therefore enforceable by:

(i) distress;

(ii) High Court or county court proceedings;

(iii) attachment of earnings;

(iv) imprisonment;

(v) other methods, eg detention for those under 21.

Where a magistrates' court on summary trial of an information makes an order for costs to be paid by the prosecutor to the accused, such order is enforceable as if it were for the payment of money recoverable summarily as a civil debt; ie by distress under MCA 1980 s.76, or in the High Court or county court under AJA 1970 s.41(3), (4). The sum may be enforced by an attachment of earnings order in the county court but not in the magistrates' court.

(c) Summary trial of either way offences

The court may order to be paid out of central government funds, the costs of the prosecution in any event; and, when the information is dismissed, the costs of the defence or of any witness for the defence for his expense, trouble or loss of time properly incurred in attending court (see *(e)* below).

The court may make orders for costs in favour of or against the prosecution or accused in the same way as it could if the case were purely summary, ie out of their own respective pockets.

In addition to the court order for prosecution costs to be paid out of central funds, it can also order payment of the whole or part to be made by the offender.

The costs are primarily payable out of central funds, when two orders are made and the Secretary of State (who pays via the justices' clerk) is entitled to be reimbursed. It is not possible for the court to make a hybrid order, eg that the offender pays £20 to the prosecutor and the balance be paid from central funds. Any order of the court must be for the whole of the prosecution costs, although an order for the offender "to pay £20 only towards the central fund expenditure" is acceptable, obviously if his means are so limited.

(d) Committal proceedings

In committal proceedings the court may order costs to paid out of central funds:

    (i) of the prosecution in any event; and

    (ii) of the defence in the event of the accused being discharged.

If there is a committal to the Crown Court, the justices' clerk ascertains the prosecution costs, and sends the certificate to the Crown Court, which pays the prosecutor that sum, or a *lesser* sum only; it cannot increase it.

(e) Awards of costs from central funds

The court has a discretionary power to order costs to be paid from the public purse — central funds. Where any award is made by the court it is dealt with by the justices' clerk for the court which makes the order, and all claims should be made through him. An application can be made after a case has been dealt with, certainly in a case withdrawn.

When the prosecution is for a serious charge, in general the prosecutor should, unless he has misconducted himself in some way, get his costs out of public funds notwithstanding that the sum involved in the charge might be trivial.

A Practice Note (see page 174) governs the award of defence costs on an acquittal. In some courts there could be some reluctance to award costs against the police, from central funds, to a successful accused. On an acquittal the defence should be able to produce and quote the Practice Note verbatim, however unexpected the acquittal might be! But see also the Practice Direction at page 175 for disallowance of costs in the Crown Court.

CCCA 1973 s.12 allows the court to order the payment out of central funds of the costs properly incurred in preparing the defence to an information charging an indictable offence but not proceeded with, together with such sums as appear reasonably sufficient to compensate any witness attending. This would cover a case "withdrawn".

(f) The amount

Prosecution: The amount awarded to compensate the prosecutor should be such amount as appears to the court reasonably sufficient to compensate him for the expenses properly incurred by him in carrying on the prosecution. It cannot be a proportion or percentage of the costs; once the court has awarded costs, it does not have to state a figure.

The amount shall be ascertained by the proper officer of the court, the justices' clerk. (The figure in the case of a salaried prosecution service may be a matter of policy, and as such an amount reached by negotiation; in other words, a fixed fee to save time-consuming taxations.)

The claim can include:

(i) advocates' fees in court as well as time spent in preparation and other expenditure necessarily incurred in bringing the matter to court, but not for a police or prison officer attending court in his capacity as such;

(ii) witnesses' "compensation" (see Costs in Criminal Cases (Allowances) Regulations 1977): this consists of compensation for witnesses attending court, for expense, trouble and loss of time properly incurred in or incidental to his attendance. Maximum rates are determined by the Lord Chancellor, with the consent of the Minister for the Civil Service, and promulgated from time to time, under reference JC (82) followed by the number.

Witnesses may be classified as:

● *Professional witnesses*, ie witnesses practising as members of the legal or medical profession or as a dentist or veterinary surgeon, who may claim for attending to give professional evidence. Note that other established professions (eg accountants) are not included. The maximum daily rate is presently (April 1986) £92.20 for over 6 hours; £69.10 for 4−6 hours;

● *Expert evidence witnesses:* witnesses giving expert evidence may claim under r.6 of the 1977 Regulations such amount as the court may consider reasonable having regard to the nature and difficulty of the case and the work reasonably involved. The amount is discretionary and unlimited;

● *Other witnesses* can claim for loss of earnings (the maximum daily rate is presently (April 1986) £24 for over four hours); subsistence allowance; night allowance; actual train or bus fare (second class only unless the court otherwise directs); taxi fare in case of emergency (if not urgent, the appropriate public transport fares); private motor car or motor cycle; an ambulance for a witness suffering from a serious illness — such reasonable sum as may be incurred; an amount paid for transportation of documents.

Note: a character witness can be paid only if the court certifies that the interests of justice require his attendance.

Defence: the amount awarded to compensate the accused should consist of such sums as appear to the court reasonably sufficient to compensate him for the expenses properly incurred by him in carrying on the defence, and to compensate any witness for his trouble or loss of time properly incurred in or incidental to his attendance. Once the court has exercised its discretion to award costs it has no further discretion to limit the amount awarded. But the court may disallow costs which are not properly incurred, eg for wasted hearings or unnecessary adjournments.

Costs to witnesses are such sums as appear reasonably sufficient to compensate any witness for the defence for the expense, trouble or loss of time incurred in or incidental to his attendance.

On the principle that costs should be borne according to the justice of the case, regard must be had to the responsibility which the legal aid fund has or ought to have to an acquitted accused. Any representative of a legally aided acquitted accused has a duty to bear this in mind and bring the fact that he is legally aided to the notice of the court, and in so doing make the appropriate application for an award of costs out of central funds, or against the prosecution according to the nature of the case, so the costs go to offset legal aid expenditure.

The amount of costs ordered to be paid shall be ascertained as soon as practicable by the proper officer of the court, normally the justices' clerk. It is sometimes practicable to award costs by a fixed sum in court. The court may ask the justices' clerk (if he is present) if he thinks this appropriate, whereupon the court may make the award; but the matter is not free from doubt where one of the justices' clerk's assistants is acting as court clerk.

Any award of costs to witnesses in the categories included above shall be on the same basis and in accordance with the same maxima mentioned above (page 85).

(g) Interpreters

A fixed sum is payable determined by the Lord Chancellor if the Welsh language is translated; otherwise the sum is at the discretion of the court. Thus interpreters can always be paid from central funds in any criminal case, summary or indictable.

(h) Prosecution of Offences Act 1985

This may well come into force 1 October 1986, but the implementing order has not been made at the date of publication.

Defendant's costs order: Where:

    (i)   an information laid before a justice of the peace for any area, charging any person with an offence, is not proceeded with;

    (ii) a magistrates' court inquiring into an indictable offence as examining justices determines not to commit the accused for trial;

    (iii) a magistrates' court dealing summarily with an offence dismisses the information;

that court may make an order for payment to be made out of central funds in favour of the accused, for his costs, and that will be called a "defendant's costs order". "Central funds" means State money, the taxpayer.

Where a person convicted of an offence by a magistrates' court appeals to the Crown Court, and in consequence of the decision on appeal:

    (i)   his conviction is set aside; or

    (ii) a less severe punishment is awarded;

the Crown Court may make a defendant's costs order in favour of the accused. The right to get costs out of public funds for an accused who merely has his sentence reduced a little on appeal is entirely new.

A defendant's costs order provides for payment to the person in whose favour the order is made of such amount as the court considers reasonably sufficient to compensate him for any expenses properly incurred by him in the proceedings. However, if there are circumstances which lead the court to the opinion that it would be inappropriate for the person in whose favour the order is made to recover the full amount, then the court must:

    (i)   assess what amount would, in its opinion, be just and reasonable, and

    (ii) specify that amount in the order.

Legal aid expenses already incurred shall be disregarded in assessing these expenses.

The amount of money to be paid out following a defendant's costs order shall:

(i) be specified in the order where the court considers it appropriate for the amount to be specified, and the person in whose favour the order is made agrees with the amount (this is brand new); and

(ii) in any other case, be determined in accordance with Regulations which the Lord Chancellor will make.

When a person is ordered to be re-tried, possibly where two magistrates disagree, and is then acquitted at his re-trial, the defendant's costs order may include the costs which might have been incurred at the original trial, as though he were there acquitted. If no order was made in respect of his expenses on appeal, the court can order any sums for the payment of which such an order could have been made.

Prosecution costs: The court can order payment out of central funds of such amount as the court considers reasonably sufficient to compensate the prosecutor for his expenses, properly incurred:

(i) in any proceedings in respect of an indictable offence; and

(ii) in any proceedings before a Divisional Court of the Queen's Bench Division or the House of Lords in respect of a summary offence;

BUT no order can be made in favour of a public authority, or a person acting on behalf of a public authority or in his capacity as an official appointed by such an authority. "Public authority" is defined in s.17(6): in effect, this means that the private prosecutor might still get his costs out of central funds for indictable offences, but public authorities will normally have to pay their own prosecution costs, subject to what follows.

Costs against the accused: A court will be able to make such order for costs to be paid by the accused to the prosecutor as it considers just and reasonable, where:

(i) any person is convicted of an offence before a magistrates' court;

(ii) the Crown Court dismisses an appeal against such a conviction or against the sentence imposed on that conviction; or

(iii) any person is convicted of an offence before the Crown Court.

Similar provisions are applicable to Court of Appeal Crown Court level cases.

However, a person under 17 years of age, found guilty of an offence before a magistrates' court, shall not be ordered to pay costs exceeding the amount of any fine imposed upon him.

Where there is a conviction in a magistrates' court and the court orders payment of any sums as a fine penalty or as compensation, and the sum ordered to be paid does not exceed £5, then the accused shall not be ordered to pay costs, unless in the particular circumstances of the case it considers it right to do so.

The Act bristles with delegated powers to the Lord Chancellor to make Regulations, to an extent that is almost unlimited. For example, to allow a court to make a costs order at any time during the proceedings. This will be brand new. Further, to compensate witnesses, interpreters, and professional medical practitioner witnesses or report makers. It is thought those Regulations will follow the existing Regulations, but then be updated from time to time to follow inflation. But there is power, it is thought, for the Lord Chancellor to make Regulations to allow costs out of central funds to an acquitted accused who faces only summary offences. This would be new, but it is thought will only be enacted when the financial climate is better than existing. Solicitors and barristers may not be keen on the provision that allows the Lord Chancellor to fix fees for legal work.

2. Civil jurisdiction

(a) Power to award costs

The power to award costs in civil proceedings is contained in MCA 1980 s.64. The court's power to order costs is discretionary; as such it must be exercised judicially. Where a complaint is proved, and an order made, an order may also be made for costs to be paid by the defendant to the complainant.

Care proceedings under the C&YPA 1969 do not permit awards of costs either way as the proceedings are not by way of complaint but by application (*R* v *Salisbury and Tisbury and Mere Combined Juvenile Court ex parte Ball* (1985)).

Where the complainant is unsuccessful, costs may be ordered against the complainant to the defendant.

It is appropriate to award costs to a successfully legally aided person in domestic proceedings. Where the losing party is legally aided and the successful party is not, the court may order costs to be paid to the latter out of the legal aid fund (LAA 1974 s.13).

If the complaint is for an order for periodical payment of money, or the revocation, revival or variation of such an order, or the enforcement of such an order, the court may, whatever adjudication it makes, order either party to pay the whole or any part of the other's costs. This provision applies equally to applications for revocation, variation or revival of a matrimonial or interim order as if it were an order for periodical payment of money.

The court may make such order as to costs as it thinks just and reasonable. It should not be in excess of the proper costs incurred — not a "penalty in disguise" case.

(b) Fixing the amount

The amount of any costs ordered to be paid in civil proceedings is to be fixed by the court as part of the adjudication. It may comprise expenses of the complainant's witnesses as well as a fee for his solicitor. Any party making an application for costs under these provisions should be able to give the court clear information of the amounts involved.

(c) Enforcement of costs

Costs awarded on a complaint for an affiliation order, or order enforceable as such; or for the enforcement, variation, discharge, revocation or revival of such an order against the person liable to make payments under the order; are enforceable as a sum ordered to be paid by an affiliation order (see page 79). Costs awarded in civil proceedings other than for orders enforceable as affiliation orders are enforceable as a civil debt in accordance with MCA 1980 s.58 (see page 58).

Chapter 8

Road traffic

1. Introduction

Contravention of road traffic law accounts for a substantial part of a magistrates' court workload, some 50% or more. Statutes and regulations governing the use of a vehicle on a road are extensive, the breach of which can have serious consequences for the person who would never ordinarily fall foul of the criminal law.

There is no special procedure governing the trial of road traffic offences. Exactly the same principles apply as described in Chapters 2 and 4.

2. Offences

Road traffic offences can be divided into 2 categories — offences involving discretionary or obligatory disqualification for driving ("endorsable" offences); and offences not involving discretionary or obligatory disqualification ("non-endorsable" offences).

(a) Non-endorsable offences

These are offences where, following a conviction, details *will not* be endorsed on the offender's driving licence.

(b) Endorsable offences

These are offences where, following a conviction, details *will* (normally) be endorsed on the offender's driving licence, or if he is not the holder of a driving licence, on any licence which he may subsequently obtain. Only a British licence can be endorsed. A "foreign" licence cannot be endorsed, but details of any endorsement ordered will be notified to the DVLC. Endorsement and disqualification must be ordered with a probation order, conditional discharge or absolute discharge as though they were convictions (RTA 1972 s.102). The details which will be endorsed will be particulars of the conviction together with particulars of disqualification or, if not disqualified, particulars of the penalty points required pursuant to s.19 TA 1981. Most endorsements remain on the licence for 4 years. But in the case of a conviction for driving or attempting to drive when unfit through drink or drugs; driving or attempting to drive with alcohol level over the limit; or driving or attempting to drive and failing to provide a specimen for analysis, the endorsement remains on the licence for 11 years. In all other cases any endorsement will remain on the licence for 4 years after the commission of the offence or until an order of disqualification is made. See Table 4, page 186 for a list of endorsable offences, maximum penalties and DoE Codes.

3. Penalty points

Since the introduction of the Transport Act 1981 conviction for an endorsable offence and endorsement results in the mandatory imposition of a prescribed number of penalty points. There can be no penalty points when a period of disqualification is ordered.

In the majority of cases the prescribed number of points to be endorsed is fixed and it is not within the court's power to vary the number of points to be endorsed. In certain cases (see Table 4, page 186) the number of points to be endorsed is variable, ie the points to be endorsed fall within a given range. It is within the court's discretion to endorse any number of points within that range. It is advisable for an offender, or his advocate, to write to the court or even appear in court in these cases, in an attempt to minimize the number of points imposed as it could have an important bearing on the question of a later possible disqualification.

Where a person is convicted of two or more offences committed on the same occasion, and the offender is not disqualified, the number of points to be endorsed is the number or highest number that would be endorsed on a conviction for any one of those offences (TA 1981 s.19(1)). For example:

Two or more offences committed on same occasion	Points	Total to be imposed for multiple offences
Example A		
defective tyre	3	
defective brakes	3	3
Example B		
defective tyre	3	
defective brakes	3	
taking vehicle		8
without consent	8	
Example C		
defective tyre	3	
defective brakes	3	within the range 4−8
no insurance	4−8	

4. Disqualification

The court has a power to disqualify an offender "for holding or obtaining a licence to drive a motor vehicle on a road" on the conviction of any endorsable offence. These are the correct words, but they are often paraphrased to "disqualified for driving" ("for" not "from"). An order for disqualification has the effect of revoking any licence from the beginning of the period of disqualification, and any licence obtained by a person who is disqualified shall be of no effect (RTA 1972 s.98).

An offender cannot be disqualified in his absence, unless a solicitor appears in court on his behalf or he has been notified, following an adjournment, of the court's intention to consider disqualification.

Periods of disqualification cannot be ordered to run consecutively to each other.

An offender can face disqualification in four ways:

(a) Obligatory disqualification

For all the offences marked in column 3 of the Table (see page 186) a court must disqualify for the fixed minimum statutory period unless there are special reasons for not doing so. If special reasons are found, 4 penalty points are imposed instead.

The length of disqualification can never be mitigated below the period fixed by law, but it can be extended.

(b) Discretionary disqualification

On conviction of any endorsable offence not subject to obligatory disqualification, the court always has a discretionary power to disqualify for such period as the court thinks fit. As a rule disqualification should be reserved for those cases involving bad driving, persistent motoring offences or where the vehicle is used for the purpose of crime: *R* v *Cooper* (1983).

(c) Disqualification pursuant to s.19 Transport Act 1981

This is disqualification for repeated offences. Where a person convicted of an offence involving obligatory or discretionary disqualification has accumulated 12 or more points, the court must disqualify for the minimum relevant period.

Calculating points to be taken into account: To determine whether the offender has accumulated 12 or more points, the points to be taken into account on the occasion of his conviction are:

(i) any that on that occasion will be ordered to be endorsed on any licence held by him or would be so ordered if he were not then ordered to be disqualified; and

(ii) any that were on a previous occasion ordered to be so endorsed,

unless the offender has since that occasion, and before the conviction, been disqualified whether pursuant to TA 1981 s.19(2), or RTA 1972 s.93, ie any period of disqualification has the effect of wiping the points slate clean.

Points endorsed in respect of any offence committed more than 3 years before the current offence are not to be taken into account when calculating the relevant number of points.

Example: X is convicted on 1 February 1986 of an offence of taking a vehicle without consent, an offence committed on 1 January 1986. His licence discloses the following:

Date of conviction	Offence	Date of offence	Points	
2.2.82	defective tyre	2.1.82	3	(A)
2.2.83	defective tyre	2.1.83	3	(B)
31.1.86	defective brakes	2.1.86	3	(C)

The points to be considered are the 8 points that would be imposed for the current offence together with the points previously imposed for offences B & C. Offence C was committed after the current offence but the points in respect of that offence are points that were ordered to be endorsed on a previous *occasion* and therefore must be taken into account. Offence A was committed more than 3 years before the current offence.

Relevant period of disqualification under s.19: Once the number of points to be considered totals 12 or more the court must disqualify for the minimum relevant period. The minimum relevant period is:

    (i)   6 months if there is no previous disqualification to take into account;

    (ii) 1 year if one previous disqualification is to be taken into account;

    (iii) 2 years if 2 or more disqualifications are to be taken into account.

A disqualification is only to be taken into account for these purposes if it was imposed within the 3 years immediately preceding the *commission* of the latest offence (TA 1981 s.19(4)).

Mitigating disqualification pursuant to s.19: The offender must be disqualified for a minimum period as calculated above unless there are grounds for mitigating the normal consequences of the conviction, in which case the offender may be disqualified for a shorter period, or not at all. When mitigating grounds are being put forward evidence should be given on oath in support.

In deciding whether or not there are grounds to mitigate the minimum period of disqualification the court must *disregard*:

    (i)   any circumstances that are alleged to make the offence, or any of the offences, not a serious one (the triviality of the offence);

    (ii) hardship, other than exceptional hardship;

    (iii) any circumstances which within the 3 years immediately preceding the conviction have already been taken into account as mitigating circumstances. The effect of this is to prevent the repeated use of an old excuse to avoid the normal consequences of repeated offending.

    (TA 1981 s.19(6)).

The court when exercising its power to mitigate the minimum period of disqualification must state its reasons for doing so in open court and these reasons must be entered in the court register (RTA 1972 s.105).

To ascertain whether mitigating circumstances have already been taken into account the court will need to have before it its own register or certified extracts from any other court's register.

(d) Disqualification until test passed

Where a person has been convicted of an endorsable offence the court may order him to be disqualified until he passes a test of competence to drive (RTA 1972 s.93(7)). This may be ordered whether or not any other disqualification has been ordered under any of the provisions of the 1972 Act or TA 1981 s.19.

If no other period of disqualification is ordered, or that period of disqualification has expired, a provisional driving licence may then be applied for to enable the offender to pass the test. If any of the conditions of a provisional licence are subsequently contravened, eg driving without supervision, it has been said that that may amount to driving whilst disqualified: *Hunter* v *Coombs* (1962).

(e) Appeal against disqualification

A person may appeal against an order for disqualification in the same manner as against a conviction. Any court in England and Wales may, if it thinks fit, suspend the disqualification pending the appeal against the order. Service of a notice of appeal is not sufficient of itself to suspend the operation of any disqualification: *Kidner* v *Daniels* (1910).

(f) Removal of disqualification

An offender who has been disqualified may in certain circumstances apply to the court by which the order was made for removal of the disqualification (RTA 1972 s.95).

The offender may not apply if he is disqualified for 2 years or less, or if he is disqualified, until he has passed a test.

He may apply:

    (i)   on the expiration of 2 years from the date the order for disqualification was made, if disqualified for less than 4 years;

    (ii) on the expiration of one half the period of disqualification, if disqualified for less than 10 years;

    (iii) on the expiration of 5 years, in any other case.

In determining the expiration of the period after which the offender may apply for the removal of disqualification, any time after conviction during which disqualification was suspended, or he was not disqualified, shall be disregarded.

If an application for removal is unsuccessful a further application can be made on the expiration of 3 months from the date of refusal.

(g) Special reasons

A court must normally order a licence to be endorsed with points and the imposition of any obligatory period of disqualification. There is a very limited discretion not to do so when the existence of a *special reason* is found. The existence of a special reason merely enables the court to exercise its discretion not to endorse or disqualify: it does not impose a duty on the court to exercise its discretion. The court's discretion should only be exercised in "clear and compelling circumstances": *Vaughan* v *Dunn* (1984). Where the court exercises its discretion in a case involving obligatory disqualification it may order a lesser period or no period of disqualification at all. Where the court exercises its discretion not to endorse then no penalty points are incurred either; no endorsement equals no penalty points. For a reason to be special it must fulfil four requirements:

(i) it must be a mitigating or extenuating circumstance;

(ii) it must not amount in law to a defence to the charge;

(iii) it must be directly connected with the commission of the offence;

(iv) the circumstance must be one which the court ought properly to take into consideration: *R* v *Wickens* (1958), as affirmed by *R* v *Jackson* (1969).

The onus is on the offender to bring himself within special reasons. The existence of a special reason should be established by evidence: *Jones* v *English* (1951). The standard of proof is on the balance of probabilities. It is not possible here to give an exhaustive list of what may or may not amount to a special reason, but the following have been held to amount to special reasons, and show the scope:

(i) the defendant was misled into committing an offence;

(ii) the shortness of the distance driven and the shortness being such that contact with other road users is unlikely: *Jones* v *Hall* (1968);

(iii) in an emergency where there is no alternative for the offender but to drive, all reasonable alternatives having been explored first.

In drink/driving cases ("laced drinks" often) it will be necessary to call expert medical evidence to establish the existence of a special reason. It is good practice for the prosecution to be notified in advance of such evidence: *Pugsley* v *Hunter* (1973). The prosecution will be allowed to test the evidence and any expert the prosecution intends to call to give evidence will normally remain in court during the giving of the defence evidence.

5. The new fixed penalty system

The imposition of a fixed penalty is a means whereby a person can avoid prosecution for a minor traffic offence by paying a fixed penalty to the justices' clerk. The new system has been enacted by TA 1982 Part III and will be effective on 1 October 1986. Schedule 1 of the Act contains a list of fixed penalty offences and, for the first time, endorsable offences are included in that list (see Table 5, page 191). An offence is not a fixed penalty offence if the offence is committed by causing or permitting a vehicle to be used by another person in contravention of any statutory provision (s.27(6)).

At the same time, fixed penalty administration is being mostly centralised at one police office in each of the 43 police forces. Additionally, one justices' clerk in each police force area (or sometimes for a county) is taking responsibility for a centralised system of taking the fixed penalty cash, and endorsing driving licences. He is called the fixed penalty clerk. The penalties will be £12 for a non-endorsable offence; £24 for an endorsable offence. The Government can increase these from time to time.

(a) Fixed penalty notice given to person present

Where a constable in uniform has reason to believe that a person is committing or has committed a fixed penalty offence he may give that person a fixed penalty notice in respect of that offence (s.27(1)). A fixed penalty notice may be issued where the person is present in respect of endorsable and non-endorsable offences. A fixed penalty notice may not be given in respect of an endorsable offence unless:

> (i) the person produces his driving licence for inspection by the constable; and
>
> (ii) the constable is satisfied that the offender would not be liable to disqualification under TA 1981 s.19(2) (disqualification for accumulation of 12 or more penalty points see page 94 above); and

(iii) the person surrenders his driving licence to the constable
to be retained and dealt with in accordance with the Act
(s.27(3)).

(b) Fixed penalty notice given at police station

Where a constable in uniform has reason to believe that a person is
committing or has committed a fixed penalty offence involving
obligatory endorsement and that person does *not* produce his
driving licence for inspection, the constable may give him a notice
stating that if the notice is produced with the driving licence at any
police station in England and Wales of the offender's choice, within
7 days, that person will then be given a fixed penalty notice in respect
of that offence (s.28(1)). This is obviously subject to the requirement that the person would not be liable to disqualification under
s.19(2) and the driving licence is surrendered as above (s.28(2)).

(c) Fixed penalty notice affixed to stationary vehicle

If a constable (he need not be in uniform) has reason to believe that
a fixed penalty offence not involving obligatory endorsement is
being or has been committed in respect of a stationary vehicle he
may affix a fixed penalty notice in respect of the offence to that
vehicle (s.27(2)).

(d) Effect of fixed penalty notice given to offender

If the fixed penalty is paid before the end of what is called the
"suspended enforcement period", no proceedings can be brought in
respect of the offence concerned (s.33(5)). The driving licence must
be endorsed by the fixed penalty clerk and returned to the licence
holder (s.34(4)).

Before the expiry of the suspended enforcement period the recipient
of the notice may give notice requiring a court hearing in respect of
the offence (s.30(2)). The matter will then be listed for court hearing
in the normal way.

The suspended enforcement period is 21 days following the date of
the notice or such longer period as may be specified in it (s.29(1)).

If a hearing has not been required and the fixed penalty remains
unpaid then a sum equal to one and a half times the amount of the
fixed penalty may be registered by the police by certificate for
enforcement against the recipient as a fine (s.30(3)). The registered
sum is enforceable as if it were a fine imposed by the registering
court on a conviction (s.36(10)). The certificate is sent to the

justices' clerk for the court area in which the defaulter appears to reside (s.36(4)). The justices' clerk there must register the sum for enforcement as a fine in his court by entering it in the court register (s.36(6)). The justices' clerk there must send notice of the registration to the defaulter (s.36(8)). The fixed penalty clerk must be informed of the registration of the sum for enforcement and upon receipt of this must endorse particulars on the licence and return it to the licence holder. If the fixed penalty clerk is the justices' clerk registering the sum for enforcement he must endorse and return the driving licence on registration of that sum (s.34(5)). Within 21 days of receipt of the notice of registration (fixed penalty plus 50%) the recipient can make and serve a statutory declaration (s.37(1)), stating, if it be the case that either (a) he was not the person to whom the fixed penalty notice was given, or (b) that he gave notice requesting a hearing before the end of the suspended enforcement period (s.37(2)). The effect of the statutory declaration is to make void the registration and any endorsement of the driving licence and, in the case of (a) above, it serves as a notice for a court hearing in respect of the offence (s.37(9)).

(e) Effect of fixed penalty fixed to vehicle

If the fixed penalty is paid before the end of the suspended enforcement period, no proceedings can be brought in respect of the offence concerned (s.33(5)).

Before the expiry of the suspended enforcement period, notice may be given requesting a hearing in respect of the offence (s.31(3)).

If the fixed penalty is not paid and a hearing has not been requested the police may serve a "notice to owner" on anyone who appears to be the owner of the vehicle (s.31(2)). The notice to owner must give particulars of the alleged offence and of the fixed penalty concerned, must state the period allowed for response and must indicate that, if the fixed penalty is not paid before the end of that period, the recipient of the notice is asked to furnish to the police a statutory statement of ownership (s.31(4)). The notice must also indicate that the person on whom it is served may either (a) give notice requesting a court hearing in respect of the offence; or (b) if he was not the driver at the time of the alleged offence and the driver wishes to give notice requesting a hearing, furnish a statutory statement of ownership together with a statutory statement of facts identifying the driver (s.32(3)).

If the recipient of the notice to owner does not respond and the fixed penalty still remains unpaid then it may be registered for enforcement as a fine as above (s.32(2)). The provisions as to the making of a statutory declaration also apply.

The recipient of the notice to owner may request a hearing in respect of the offence and proceedings may then be instituted against him. For the purpose of these proceedings it is conclusively presumed that the person on whom the notice was served was the driver at the time of the offence (s.31(7)) unless it is proved that at the time of the offence the vehicle was in the possession of a third party without the consent of the "owner" (s.31(8)).

If the recipient of such a notice was not the owner of the vehicle at the time of the offence, and he furnishes a statutory statement of ownership to that effect, he escapes liability for the offence (s.31(5)).

If the recipient of such a notice was not the driver at the time of the offence, and the person who was the driver wants a court hearing, the recipient of the notice may furnish both a statutory statement of ownership and a statutory statement of facts. This has effect as if the driver of the vehicle at the time of the offence has given notice requesting a hearing (s.32(3)).

The new system has been introduced to remedy deficiencies. Hopefully it will result in the consistent use of fixed penalties and successful enforcement of the notices issued; and overcome the procedural difficulties of the owner liability regulations contained in the Road Traffic Regulation Act, 1984. Time alone will tell if the objectives of the Act are achieved.

As a practical point, if a fixed penalty notice is issued for an endorsable offence (say, speeding), and the licence is not produced there and then, the motorist will have to produce the notice and his licence, and possibly insurance and other documents, at a police station within 7 days (see page 99). Assuming any points on the licence, including those for the current offence, do not exceed 12, the fixed penalty notice is effective and the licence will normally be endorsed with 3 points. But if the motorist has no insurance resulting in prosecution, is he to have 3 points for speeding *and* further points (4-8) if found guilty in court of the no insurance offence. The answer is no; had both cases gone to court under existing law, the points for both offences (committed on the same occasion) would be in the range 4-8 (see page 93). So, the rules when promulgated, should provide that the court, having fixed the points for the no insurance offence, will deduct the points for speeding, thus equating the situation with the current position where both matters go to court. It is not exactly clear *how* the court will know of the fixed penalty points.

Chapter 9

Legal aid

1. Availability

Legal aid is available, one way or the other, for virtually every case in a magistrates' court, except for prosecution in criminal cases. The system is somewhat patchwork, with various authorities involved, but it can be summarized as follows:

- (i) The Green Form Scheme;
- (ii) Advice at police stations;
- (iii) Criminal legal aid for proceedings;
- (iv) Matrimonial cases.

The figures quoted in this Chapter for the various limits and allowances in connection with legal aid are correct as at April 1986.

2. The Green Form Scheme

This is administered by The Law Society under LAA 1974 Part I, as amended by LAA 1979 and LAA 1982. Advice and assistance is available to any person whose disposable income does not exceed £114 per week and whose disposable capital does not exceed £800 where there are no dependants. Disposable income is the gross income of the applicant and his/her spouse, less deductions for tax, National Insurance, and dependants' allowances on a sliding scale.

Legal advice might be given by a solicitor (any solicitor chosen by the applicant), or if necessary by counsel, about English law affecting the person seeking advice, and about any steps that that person might take. Assistance can be given in taking such steps as are necessary to start or defend proceedings. The scheme is *not* to be used for advice and assistance to persons detained at a police station (see below).

The cost of the legal advice and assistance available is limited to £50 unless approval for an extension is obtained from the appropriate Area Committee of The Law Society. This can be given on the telephone in an emergency.

This assistance could include representation before a court or a tribunal but only with approval of the Area Committee, and only for (most) domestic proceedings, not for criminal cases. The magistrates' court can allow representation under the Green Form Scheme for criminal cases, but the cost limit is still £50, and the form must be so endorsed by the justices' clerk. The eligibility limit for capital is £3,000.

Assistance by way of representation under LAA 1972 s.2 is extended to persons in respect of whom a warrant of further detention or an extension of such a warrant is made under PACEA 1984 s.43 or s.49 (see page 25).

A person wishing to take advantage of these provisions must apply to the solicitor consulted, who will complete the "Green Form" and assess the applicant's means and determine any contribution which might be payable by him. The solicitor then collects that contribution and is reimbursed for any cost over and above that contribution, but within the £50 limit.

This scheme is only available when a civil legal aid certificate or a criminal legal aid order is not in force for the proceedings.

The "Green Form", which has a reference LA/Rep/6A, is reproduced at page 130.

3. Advice at police stations

PACEA 1984 provides for free legal advice and assistance to detainees at police stations, ie legal aid is available and is not means-tested. There is a cost limit for non-arrestable offences of £50, and for arrestable offences, £90. The limit for the latter can be extended by the Area Legal Aid Office retrospectively but the non-arrestable offence limit can never be extended. These limits apply whether the advice is given by the detainee's own solicitor or by a duty solicitor under the 24 hour duty solicitor scheme (Legal Aid (Duty Solicitor) Scheme 1985; see below). An enhanced payment is made to the duty solicitor in certain circumstances. The Schedule at page 148 tabulates this. The form LA/REP/12, at page 146, shows how a solicitor reports the advice given at the police station to claim his fee.

4. Legal aid in criminal proceedings and care cases

(a) Own solicitor (ie not duty solicitor)

Availability: Legal aid, including representation, is available for persons charged with an offence before a magistrates' court, or where a person appears or is brought before a magistrates' court to be dealt with. "Magistrates' court" in this context is a magistrates' court or a juvenile court. Legal aid can be granted limited to a bail application only. A "through order" can be made to cover both committal proceedings and Crown Court trial.

Legal aid, including representation, is available for a juvenile (and additionally, for a parent when an order is made that the parent shall not represent the juvenile in proceedings) who is or is about to be brought before a juvenile court in care proceedings under C&YPA 1961 s.1.

Legal aid, including representation, is available to a person, and a parent as above, the subject of an application to a magistrates' court to vary or discharge a supervision order under C&YPA 1969 s.15; for a person the subject of an application to vary or discharge a care order under C&YPA 1969 s.21; and for a person who makes an application to a magistrates' court under PCCA 1973 s.37.

Persons who are guilty of contempt in the face of a magistrates' court (as defined by Contempt of Court Act 1981 s.12) might be dealt with there and then by the magistrates' court. Section 13 of the Act provides for legal aid to be granted to such a person by the court, and not under the civil legal aid scheme.

In all these cases, the power to grant a legal aid order is vested in the magistrates' court, although payment to the solicitors involved will be made by the appropriate Area Committee of The Law Society.

An application form for what is called "criminal legal aid" is reproduced at page 134, and requires a Statement of Means form to be submitted (see page 135). Note from the forms *who* is to apply — the parent for the under-17 year olds; and who is an "appropriate contributor" for the under-16 year olds.

Applications will not normally be considered unless they are accompanied by the statement of means; these forms are normally obtainable from a magistrates' court and most police stations. The completed forms must be lodged with the court as soon as possible, even before a charge is made if it is certain that one is to be made. It is possible to make the application for legal aid in open court, but such application will usually be referred to the justices' clerk, and the better practice is to apply by lodging the forms with the court office.

Criteria for grant: The statutory criterion for grant or refusal by the court is whether or not "it is desirable to grant legal aid in the interests of justice where it appears that the person's means are such that he requires assistance in meeting the costs he may incur". Where there is doubt, it should be resolved in favour of a grant (LAA 1974 s.29).

The practicality is that the court will follow the "Widgery Criteria" and statutes which suggest that legal aid should be granted (unless the defendant's means justify refusal) if:

(i)   the charge is murder; or

(ii) where an accused who is in custody and not represented is likely to be further remanded in custody; or

(iii) the accused is likely to receive a custodial sentence (immediate or suspended); or

(iv) the charge is a grave one in the sense that the accused is in real jeopardy of losing his livelihood, or suffering serious damage to his reputation; or

(v) the charge raises a substantial question of law; or

(vi) the accused is unable to follow the proceedings and state his own case because of his inadequate knowledge of English, mental illness or other mental or physical disability; or

(vii) the nature of the defence involves the tracing and interviewing of witnesses, or expert cross-examination of a witness for the prosecution; or

(viii) legal representation is desirable in the interests of someone other than the accused, as, for example, in the case of sexual offences against young children when it is undesirable that the accused should cross-examine the witness in person.

Grant or refusal: If legal aid is granted, a certificate is drawn up by the justices' clerk and a copy sent to the accused and the solicitors concerned who will use their copy to claim their costs from The Law Society in due course. Legal aid can be granted in this context by the court, a justice of the peace, or the justices' clerk.

On a refusal, if it appears to the person involved or his solicitor that the refusal was harsh, it is a good practical operation to write to the justices' clerk inviting a review, especially if more details have become available to support the application. It is doubtful that more than one application can be made and not on remand hearings, but most courts are reasonable in not blocking a review of a refusal, on good grounds, or a further application in court in exceptional cases, particularly where there has been a change of circumstances.

Where a court has refused legal aid as not being in the interests of justice, and the offence is either indictable or triable either way, a review by the Area Legal Aid Committee can be requested. The application must be made within 14 days of the refusal and not less than 21 days before the date fixed for trial or committal. The Area Legal Aid Committee can also review a magistrates' court's refusal to grant a legal aid certificate to include counsel.

A person successfully applying for legal aid will normally be able to have the solicitor of his choice, but where there are *joint* accused, the court may assign one solicitor to act for several accused unless there is a possible conflict of interest.

Contribution orders: These require payment towards legal aid by, normally, the accused. Where there is disposable income or capital above the minima (see below) the court *must* make a contribution order at the time the legal aid order is made. The contribution is payable in one sum or by instalments, and if an instalment is not paid, the court may revoke the legal aid order. The court can grant legal aid without a Statement of Means if it appears that the offender is incapable of furnishing one because of his physical or mental condition. Instalments can be varied if the offender's means change. Payments are made to the justices' clerk.

Persons receiving supplementary benefit and those whose disposable income, ie after deductions for dependants etc, is £46 per week or less, make no contribution. Above this figure, there is a sliding scale. The allowances vary from time to time (downwards as well as upwards), thus the government can control eligibility and, more importantly, control the (part) cost to the "consumer", although the higher the contribution the more likely is the "consumer" to decline to pay and receive legal aid.

The solicitor claims his fee by using Form LA/Rep/3B, reproduced at page 142.

Restrictions: In view of a tremendous escalation of legal aid costs between 1967 and 1980, the Lord Chancellor, who now has ministerial responsibility for the administration of legal aid in criminal cases, wrote to justices' clerks on 27 March 1981 with a view to the appropriate authority (the court, a justice of the peace, or a justices' clerk) exercising greater care in the grant of legal aid. The circular is reproduced as Appendix 4, page 195.

(b) Duty solicitor scheme

In many areas a duty solicitor is in attendance at magistrates' courts.

The scheme was set up under the provisions of LAA 1974 s.15, LAA 1982 s.1 and Legal Aid (Duty Solicitor Scheme) 1983. It provides for the appointment and remuneration of solicitors to be in attendance at court to give advice and undertake representation for un-represented defendants. It is not normally available for those charged with non-imprisonable offences, for not-guilty pleas or committal proceedings. Advice and representation is available to each defendant once only on a particular charge. Defendants may still opt for advice and representation from their own solicitor either under the Green Form Scheme, a legal aid order, or at their own expense. Duty solicitors are remunerated at an hourly rate for all the time they spend at court. The scheme is not intended as a cheap alternative to "full" legal aid, and not all courts have such a system.

5. Appeals

On an appeal from a magistrates' court to a Crown Court, either against conviction or sentence, legal aid with representation is available to a convicted person, and sometimes to the prosecutor as respondent to the appeal. Advice on whether to appeal would be covered by the original legal aid order for magistrates' court proceedings.

Either the magistrates' court *or* the Crown Court can grant legal aid on application being made, and application forms are similar to those used for magistrates' court cases (see above).

If a decision of a magistrates' court (civil or criminal) is to be questioned in the High Court by case stated (see page 115) or judicial review (see page 125), legal aid is dealt with by the Area Committee of The Law Society, to whom application is made.

6. Matrimonial cases

Legal aid here is granted by the appropriate Area Committee of The Law Society to whom application should be made. The court normally has no role here either in the grant of legal aid or payment to solicitors. The form of application is reproduced at page 144, and the form indicates the types of proceedings covered.

It is unlikely that this legal aid will be available for cases involving variation of maintenance payments only, unless there are special factors involved, possibly some extreme disability of the applicant so that he cannot put his own means forward to the court.

Chapter 10

Appeals

1. Generally

There are four ways in which the decisions of magistrates and of magistrates' courts may be questioned or reviewed:

    (a) appeal to the Crown Court;
- in all criminal proceedings — by the offender on conviction;
- in some civil proceedings — by the party dissatisfied with the decision;

    (b) appeal to the High Court for magistrates to state a case — by any party aggrieved, alleging error on a question of law or jurisdiction;

    (c) appeal to the High Court (Family Division) after magistrates have given their reasons in domestic proceedings — by any of the parties to the proceedings;

    (d) application to the High Court for judicial review; it is within the ordinary powers of the High Court to exercise a controlling jurisdiction over the actions of magistrates by way of the prerogative orders of *mandamus, prohibition* and *certiorari* — by a party aggrieved.

2. The "slip rule"

There always was an inherent right in the High Court, if a mistake had been made, to put it right, and often a judge would have an offender brought back so a correct sentence, for example, was passed. A fairly recent statutory provision, MCA 1980 s.142 provides a similar "slip rule" for magistrates' courts. A court can vary or rescind a sentence or other order imposed or made by the court when dealing with an offender. A sentence can be replaced if it appears to be invalid.

Similarly, where someone is found guilty in a case where he pleaded not guilty, or the court proceeded in the absence of the accused and it appears to the court that it would be in the interest of justice that the case ought to be reheard, the court can so direct.

When that happens the original finding of guilt or sentence or order can be treated as a nullity and the case reheard.

The only restrictions on that are first, that there is a time limit of 28 days, from the date on which the sentence or order was imposed. Secondly, the decision has to be made by the same magistrates by whom the sentence or order was wrongly imposed, or if there were three or more magistrates sitting, by a majority.

It is not of common occurrence, but sometimes, to avoid the expense of an appeal to the Crown Court or elsewhere, it might be sensible to approach the justices' clerk to see if the slip rule could be used.

It would be in the interests of justice to re-hear a case (a plea of not guilty indicated) which was listed for 10 am, where a conviction had taken place between 10.00 am and 10.45 am, the accused arriving at court after 10.45 am, and even then not getting to the right court room. It would appear good practice to "put the case back a bit in the list" to avoid the problem (*R* v *Camberwell Green Magistrates' Court, ex parte Ibrahim* (1984)).

3. Appeals to the Crown Court: criminal jurisdiction

The rights of appeal to the Crown Court from magistrates' courts are purely statutory:

(a) Under MCA 1980 s.108

Appeals to the Crown Court from the decisions of magistrates' courts exercising their criminal jurisdiction may arise on conviction and on being sentenced:

    (i) *on conviction* — a person convicted by a magistrates' court may appeal:

- if he pleaded guilty, against his sentence;
- if he did not plead guilty, against both conviction and sentence;

    The situation can arise where the accused pleaded guilty originally, but in the Crown Court alleged the plea was equivocal before justices. The Crown Court must enquire into it and, if necessary, ask the justices and/or the court clerk for an affidavit dealing with what happened. It would appear the Crown Court (not the Divisional Court) is the arbiter on whether the plea was equivocal or not. If it finds the plea was equivocal, and remits the case to the magistrates' court for trial as a not guilty case, the magistrates' court must accept it and try it accordingly (*R v Plymouth Justices, ex parte Hart* (1986)). This case may not be popular with the author, and may be wrong, but it is binding! Even in the Crown Court there can be clear pleas of guilty, only to be re-opened in its appeal court, if the appellant, even with numerous convictions and legally represented, was "wholly confused . . . so his mind never really went to his plea" (*R v Phillips* (1982)).

(ii) *on being sentenced* for an offence; here "sentence" means any order made on conviction except:

- an order for payment of costs;
- an order for destruction of an animal under Protection of Animals Act 1911 s.2;
- an order made in any case where the court had no discretion as to the making of the order and its terms.

Note: there is no similar right of appeal to a Crown Court for the prosecutor. There used to be no appeal against "sentence" by probation or conditional discharge, but an appeal is now possible (CJA 1982 Sch.16).

(b) Practice

Notice of appeal: an appeal is commenced by the appellant's giving notice of the appeal in accordance with CCR 1971. See Form at page 167. MCR 1981 r.74 sets out the documents to go from the magistrates' court to the Crown Court.

The notice must be in writing and given as follows:

(i) if the appeal is against a decision of a magistrates' court, to the clerk of that court;

(ii) in any other case, to the chief clerk of the Crown Court; and

(iii) in any case, to any other party or parties to the appeal.

Note: in third party proceedings it is necessary that substantive notice of appeal be given to the original prosecutor as well as to the third party.

Notice must be given within 21 days after the day on which the decision appealed against was given, ie when the sentence or order is finally announced, but:

(i)   time for giving notice of appeal may be extended either before or after it expires, by the Crown Court; application for an extension of time is made in writing to the chief clerk of the Crown Court, specifying the grounds of the application;

(ii) where the Crown Court extends time for giving notice of appeal the appropriate officer of the Crown Court shall give notice to the appellant and the clerk of the magistrates' court; the appellant should then give notice of the extension to any other party to the appeal.

It would appear that an appellant may request a copy of the justices' clerk's notes taken in the magistrates' court, if any (*Hill* v *Wilson* (1985)); and see Legal Aid in Criminal Proceedings (General) Regulations 1968 reg. 16, for the supply of such notes, if any (or depositions) to the solicitor assigned.

Whether the justices' clerk is under a *duty* to take a note is much debated, although it is thought he must in domestic proceedings. In over-ruling a magistrates' decision that there was no case to answer in a summary case, Watkins LJ said it was incumbent on a court clerk to keep notes, though it was later qualified to read a clerk of experience, and a note of at least the main features of the evidence: *Lancashire County Council* v *Clarke* (1984).

Service of any notice of appeal may be by:

(i)   delivering it to the person to whom it is directed; or

(ii) properly addressing, pre-paying, and posting a letter containing the document.

Notice of hearing: on receiving notice of appeal the appropriate officer of the Crown Court enters the appeal and gives notice of the time and place of the hearing to the appellant, the clerk of the magistrates' court and any other party to the appeal.

Bail pending appeal: the provisions allowing bail to be granted are contained in MCA 1980 s.113. After giving notice of appeal to the Crown Court (within the normal 21 days) against a decision of a magistrates' court, if the appellant is in custody (including care in the case of a juvenile), the magistrates' court may grant him bail.

If the appellant has been convicted of an offence in criminal proceedings, the provisions of BA 1976 (except that of the general right of bail of accused persons) will apply. If the proceedings are other than criminal, the appellant may be required to enter into a recognizance with or without sureties. The time and place at which the appellant is to appear will be the appointed time for the hearing at the Crown Court.

If bail is withheld an unrepresented appellant should be told that he may apply further for bail to the Crown Court or High Court.

If the magistrates refuse bail:

(i) an unrepresented appellant must be told of his right to apply to the Crown Court for bail;

(ii) the appellant may apply to the Crown Court in any event.

Suspension of driving disqualification pending appeal: a magistrates' court which makes an order disqualifying an offender for driving may suspend the disqualification pending an appeal against the order. The court which suspends a disqualification in this way must notify the Secretary of State (DVLC) of the suspension.

Any period of suspension of disqualification is disregarded in calculating the period of disqualification.

The Crown Court has power to suspend the disqualification in the same way as the magistrates' court.

Written notice of appeal against the disqualification must be served before making an application for the disqualification to be suspended.

(c) Powers of Crown Court at the hearing

The appeal is by way of rehearing. The Crown Court (unless the statute relating to the appeal limits the court's powers) may:

(i) correct any error or mistake in the order or judgment;

(ii) confirm, reverse or vary the decision appealed against;

(iii) remit the matter with its opinion (possibly binding upon the magistrates) to the magistrates;

(iv) make any other order as the court thinks just and exercise any power which the magistrates' court had, including the power to award any punishment, whether more or less severe than that awarded by the magistrates' court.

This is exactly opposite to the rights of the Court of Appeal (Criminal Division) hearing appeals against sentence by a Crown Court, which cannot increase the sentence.

However, a Crown Court may not substitute a conviction for an attempt to commit the offence, on appeal against conviction for the offence: *R* v *Manchester Crown Court, ex parte Hill* (1985).

(d) Effect of decision on appeal

On the determination by the Crown Court of the appeal, by confirmation, variation or substitution, the decision may be enforced in the same way that it could have been in the magistrates' court; and the decision of the Crown Court shall have effect as if it had been made by the magistrates' court against which the appeal was brought.

(e) Abandonment of appeal

Notice to abandon: The Crown Court itself may give leave for the appeal to be abandoned; otherwise to be effective, notice to abandon must comply with the following conditions:

(i)   it must be in writing;

(ii) it must be given not later than the third day before the day fixed for hearing the appeal (Saturdays, Sundays and public holidays excepted);

(iii) it must be given to:

- the clerk to the magistrates' court from which the appeal was made;
- any other party or parties to the appeal;
- the appropriate officer of the Crown Court;
- in the case of an appeal under Licensing Act 1964 s.21, to the clerk of the licensing justices.

Abandonment of appeal in accordance with these conditions will normally avoid an order for costs of the respondent being made against the appellant.

Consequences of abandonment: Where notice to abandon the appeal has been properly given, the court against whose decision the appeal was brought may:

(i)   issue enforcement process subject to any enforcement steps which may have been taken previously;

(ii) on the application of any party to the appeal order the appellant to pay the other party's reasonable costs.

An appeal abandoned may not be "unabandoned".

4. Appeals to the Crown Court: civil jurisdiction

Other orders of magistrates' courts may be the subject of separate statutory rights of appeal, eg under:

(a) Magistrates' Courts (Appeal from Binding Over Orders) Act 1956 (see below);

(b) Affiliation Proceedings Act 1957 (see below);

(c) Licensing Act 1964.

(a) Appeals from binding over orders

Appeals to the Crown Court against an order of binding over of a magistrates' court, whether under the Justices of the Peace Act 1361 or otherwise, are permitted under Magistrates' Courts (Appeals from Binding Over Orders) Act 1956 s.1.

CCR 1971 apply to service and the form of notice (see page 110). The respondent to the appeal is the other party (who may be a witness or otherwise) to the proceedings.

Bail pending appeal may be granted (see page 42), and legal aid (see page 104) may be allowed to both parties.

(b) Appeals under Affiliation Proceedings Act 1957

Appeals to the Crown Court in relation to affiliation orders are permitted as follows:

(i) on the making or refusal to make such an order;

(ii) on the revocation, revival or variation of such an order;

(iii) on *quantum* only: *R* v *Hereford Justies, ex parte O.* (1983).

Note: there is no right of appeal against a refusal to revive; or against an order made on complaint for the enforcement of an order. These go to the High Court.

CCR 1971 regarding service and form of notice apply (see page 110). The respondent to the appeal will be the other party to the application for the affiliation order in the magistrates' court. The order is to be considered as made when the decision is announced in the magistrates' court and errors in the order as drawn up are not grounds for appeal. The order may be bad in part and good for the residue.

5. Other rights of appeal

There are other rights of appeal from decisions of magistrates to the

Crown Court conferred by statute, eg under the betting and gaming legislation and under the Licensing Act 1964. Specific provisions relating to that type of appeal are set out in the specific statute. Beware an appeal against a care order, eg C&YPA 1969 s.15. If the juvenile court has made an order that the parent should not represent the child in care proceedings, that might prevent the parent appealing on behalf of the child (C&YPA 1969 s.32A).

6. Appeals to the High Court: case stated

(a) Authority to appeal

Under MCA 1980 s.111, any person who was a party to the proceedings before a magistrates' court, or who is aggrieved by the conviction, order, determination or other proceedings of the court, may question it on the ground that it is wrong in law or in excess of jurisdiction, by applying to the justices to state a case for the opinion of the High Court on the question. A magistrates' court has no jurisdiction to state a case unless and until a final determination of the case has been made: *Streames* v *Copping* (1985).

Generally the case will be heard by a Divisional Court of the Queen's Bench Division; but a Divisional Court of the Family Division has jurisdiction in appeals against an order or determination of a magistrates' court with regard to the enforcement of an order made under DPMCA 1978 Part I, some registered orders, some affiliation proceedings and so on.

(b) Who can appeal

The right to appeal extends to:

(i)   any of the parties to the proceedings including the prosecutor in a case which has been dismissed (his only remedy really);

(ii) any other person aggrieved, eg a person who is dissatisfied with the incompleteness of his success in the destruction of obscene articles; or who is adversely affected by the decision but was not a party to the proceedings; this will include a party or parties joined in the proceedings as third parties, under for example, s.113, Food and Drugs Act 1955.

(c) Grounds for appeal

(i)   wrong in law — examples are:

- where justices come to a decision to which no reasonable bench could come, but not so as to reverse an acquittal in criminal proceedings, which can be the result of judicial review: *R* v *Dorking Justices, ex parte Harrington* (1983).

- indefensible decisions as to legal conclusions;

(ii) excess of jurisdiction — examples are:

- completion of a case when the court had no jurisdiction to try it;

- *ultra vires* decisions of magistrates, eg passing a sentence more severe than the law allows. And a case stated procedure can be used for a lawful, albeit severe, sentence if it is alleged the sentence is harsh or oppressive or so far outside the normal discretionary limits that it could be said the imposition must involve an error of law somewhere: *Universal Salvage Ltd & Robinson* v *Boothby* (1984).

(d) Mode of appeal

Notice (MCR 1981 rr.76-81): Application to state a case must be:

(i) made within 21 days after the day on which the decision was given or sentence fully announced. The High Court has no power to extend the period. (The High Court will sometimes decline to hear a case which has not been concluded by the justices; it will not decide an academic question);

(ii) made in writing, signed by the appellant or his solicitor and delivered or sent by post (by registered or recorded delivery service) to the clerk to the magistrates' court whose decision is questioned (mistakes in the names of the justices are irrelevant);

(iii) drawn so as to identify the question or questions of law or jurisdiction on which the opinion of the High Court is sought, in compliance with MCR 1981 r.76. This is a condition precedent to appeals by case stated; consequently if the notice does not sufficiently identify the question of law or jurisdiction, the justices need not state the case. Hence, care should be taken to particularise the essential points of the appeal upon which the opinion of the High Court is sought, since the case which is to be stated by the justices will be directed to the question or questions contained therein. Whether a failure to identify the question of law or jurisdiction is fatal to the application will depend on the circumstances of the application, and whether there has been a substantial compliance with r.76.

Time considerations: by MCR 1981 r.77, a draft is to be prepared and a copy sent by the justices' clerk to all the parties to the appeal within 21 days of the application. The parties may then make representations which must be submitted within 21 days of receipt of the draft, to the justices' clerk, for the consideration of the justices stating the case. Within a further period of 21 days the case is to be formally stated and signed by the justices, or the justices' clerk on their behalf.

The time limits are directory, not mandatory, and may be extended by the justices' clerk under r.79, but an explanation must be given before he will exercise that right.

Contents of the case: the draft case must follow a prescribed form (see MC(F)R 1981 Form 155 and MCR 1981 r.81 and page 118). It must state:

(i) *particulars of offence:* the date of hearing and particulars of the information or complaint, ie the words of the summons or charge must be specified;

(ii) *the facts:* facts which were found proved by the justices, or admitted, should be stated individually, generally in numbered paragraphs. When stating the facts found, statements of the evidence given are irrelevant and should not be included. If a respondent contends that certain facts found by the justices have been omitted from the case he can apply to the High Court for a reassessment of the case on stating in an affidavit the findings of fact which in his opinion have been omitted;

(iii) *evidence:* a short statement of the evidence is only appropriate in cases in which the opinion of the High Court is sought as to whether there was evidence on which the magistrates' court could come to its decision; in this case the particular finding of fact which it is claimed cannot be supported by the evidence must be stated in the notice of appeal;

(iv) *contention of appellant and respondent:* the contentions of both (or all) parties to the appeal should be stated in brief paragraphs summarising the points made by them respectively;

(v)   *cited cases:* it is necessary to list the cases (if any) which were referred to during the hearing, to enable the High Court to consider them also;

(vi) *the opinion:* a paragraph or paragraphs concluding the case must state the opinion held by the justices in their deliberations. The grounds which they had for coming to their decision are included in this part of the case;

(vii) *the decision:* the paragraph or paragraphs of the decision are stated as a consequence of the facts found, and the opinion held by the justices in the case. They will contain the matters which will be of particular importance and interest to the High Court;

(viii)*the sentence or order:* the sentence or order of the court must be stated with all other orders and ancillary matters particularised, eg endorsement, compensation orders, costs, legal aid etc;

(ix) *the question:* the question for the opinion of the High Court will be decided by the justices themselves, though in most cases it will be the question or questions posed by the appellant in his notice requesting a case to be stated.

Draft case: an application complying with r.76 must be sent to the clerk of the justices as stated in para (i) on page 116, whereupon he will prepare a draft case immediately (unless the justices are likely to refuse to state a case). The draft will follow the content and form outlined above so that representations can be made.

Representations on the draft may be made by any of the parties to the appeal within the time limits set out on page 117 (MCR 1981 r.77(2)). Representations must be in writing and signed by or on behalf of the party making them and sent to the justices' clerk. In difficult cases the parties may discuss the case informally with the justices' clerk.

The justices' clerk, immediately after the expiry of the date upon which representations may be made by the parties, should make them available to the justices and agree a final form of the case. This must then be signed by two or more of the justices, or the justices' clerk on their behalf, and sent to the parties, again within 21 days.

It is irrelevant that the decision was by a majority, and no note is made of any dissenting justice.

Lodging the case: where a case has been stated by the justices, the appellant must within 10 days after receipt lodge the original and three copies of it in the Crown Office (or the Principal Registry of the Family Division, as the case may be); and within 4 days after lodging the case serve a notice of the entry of the appeal, together with a copy of the case, on the respondent.

Unless the court having jurisdiction to determine the appeal directs otherwise, the appeal shall not be heard sooner than 8 days after service of the notice of entry of appeal. Regard should be had to these time limits, as costs may be incurred if they are ignored; application for extension of time limits may be made by two clear days' notice of motion to the Divisional Court, supported by affidavit.

(e) Powers of High Court on appeal

The court has power by s.7, Summary Jurisdiction Act 1857 to send the case back to the justices for amendment; though, if the amendment is on the question of the omission of facts the appellant should apply before the hearing, by a two-day motion, asking for the case to be sent back for restatement. Under s.6 of this Act the High Court hears the case; one counsel on either side is allowed. The justices will not normally be heard except by affidavit under the Review of Justices' Decisions Act 1872. Occasionally, though, the justices themselves may be represented. The High Court may:

(i) determine the question or questions of law arising, and may reverse, affirm or amend the determination in respect of which the case has been stated; or

(ii) remit the case to the justices with the opinion of the court thereon (which will be binding on the justices); or

(iii) make such other order in relation to the case as it deems fit; and

(iv) make any order as to costs, at discretion.

All such cases shall be final and conclusive, subject only to appeal to the House of Lords under the Administration of Justice Act 1960.

Costs usually follow the event, but they are not generally given against an unsuccessful respondent who does not appear, unless he took and made the point the subject of the appeal in the magistrates' court; costs cannot normally be ordered against the erring justices, but there are rare exceptions where the justices acted unreasonably and perversely.

(f) Enforcement of decision

Any conviction, order, determination or other proceedings of a magistrates' court varied, or any judgment or order on appeal by case stated, may be enforced as if it were a decision of the magistrates' court.

(g) Frivolous appeals

If the justices are of the opinion that an application to state a case is frivolous, they may refuse to state a case; whereupon they must give the applicant a certificate to that effect if required; where the applicant is the Attorney General the justices cannot decline to state a case as being frivolous.

Where justices refuse as above, the High Court may, on the appellant's applying for the case to be stated, make an order of *mandamus* requiring the justices to state it (see page 125).

(h) Effect on right of appeal to Crown Court

On the making of an application to state a case, the right of the applicant to appeal against the decision to the Crown Court ceases.

(i) Bail pending appeal

Similar provisions allowing the applicant to apply for bail exist in appeals to the Divisional Court as they do to appellants to the Crown Court (see page 111).

(j) Legal aid to appeal to High Court

Legal aid for appeals by way of case stated falls within Part I, LAA 1974 (s.7 and Sched. 1). Applications for such legal aid certificates are made to The Law Society; see page 107.

(k) Recognizance to prosecute the appeal

Justices who have been asked to state a case may require the applicant, before stating it, to enter into a recognizance with or without sureties before the magistrates' court, guaranteeing that he will prosecute the appeal, submit to the judgment of the High Court, and pay the costs of the appeal. The recognizance may be required at any time before the case is stated, but is not obligatory. The amount of the recognizance, and the necessity for sureties is entirely within the court's discretion.

7. Appeals to the High Court (RSC 1965 O.55)

(a) Authority to appeal

Statutory rights of appeal to the High Court against magistrates' courts' decisions are provided in seven cases, in accordance with the provisions of RSC 1965 O.55, namely:

(i) Guardianship of Minors Act 1975 s.16(3);

(ii) Children Act 1975 s.101(2);

(iii) Children Act 1948 s.4A;

(iv) Maintenance Orders Act 1968 s.4(7);

(v) Magistrates' Courts Act 1980 s.63(3);

(vi) Domestic Proceedings and Magistrates' Courts Act 1978 s.29;

(vii)Matrimonial Proceedings (Magistrates' Courts) Act 1960.

The procedure on appeals under these sections is contained in RSC 1965 OO.16 and 90.

Note, oddly, that an appeal lies under (vi) above, against a magistrates' court order to vary or otherwise a periodical maintenance payment, but an order to remit arrears or otherwise has to be appealed by case stated: *Fletcher* v *Fletcher* (1985).

(b) Judicial review and case stated

The ordinary jurisdiction of the High Court to examine the proceedings of magistrates' courts by judicial review is not affected by the above provisions; but an appeal by case stated is not a valid form of appeal in these cases, save upon a point of law arising from proceedings in the magistrates' court.

(c) Court to hear appeal

Appeals brought under O.55 are assigned to the Divisional Court and are heard and determined:

(i) where the decision of the High Court is final, by a Divisional Court;

(ii) in any other case, by a single judge.

(d) Appeals in domestic cases

Justices' reasons: as a preliminary to giving notice of appeal, and to enable him to make any necessary application for legal aid, a party wishing to appeal may request the justices' clerk to supply the justices' reasons for their decision. In an appeal concerning a child, an application may be made to a judge of the Family Division if there is difficulty in obtaining reasons or documents.

The document containing justices' reasons should contain the following:

(i) the names of the justices at the head;

(ii) particulars of the facts found proved, using clear terms as to acts of cruelty;

(iii) the justices' view as to the personalities of the parties concerned;

(iv) the reasons upon which the justices reached their conclusions, together with the cases considered;

(v) the signatures of the justices and an explanation of the absence of any signature;

(vi) if one justice dissents this must be stated but his reasons cannot be demanded.

Procedure: RSC 1965 O.90 r.16 lays down the procedure in appeals under MP(MC)A 1960 or DPMCA 1978. It requires:

(i) every such appeal to be heard and determined by a Divisional Court;

(ii) every such appeal to be entered by lodging three copies of the notice of motion in the Principal Registry;

(iii) notice of motion need not be served in accordance with O.65 r.5(i);

(iv) on entering the appeal or as soon as practicable thereafter the appellant to lodge in the Principal Registry:

- three certified copies of the summons and the order appealed against, and of any order staying its execution;

- three copies of the justices' clerk's notes of evidence (produced in double spaced typing);

- three copies of the justices' reasons for their decision;

- a certificate that the notice of motion has been duly served on the justices' clerk and every other party affected by the appeal;

- where an application to extend the time for bringing the appeal is included in the notice of motion, a certificate and a copy thereof, by the appellant or his solicitor, of the reasons for the delay.

The hearing: if the justices' clerk's notes are not produced the court may hear and determine the appeal on any other evidence or statement of what occurred in the magistrates' court.

The court is not bound to allow the appeal on the ground merely of a misdirection or improper reception or rejection of evidence, unless a miscarriage of justice is apparent.

A registrar may dismiss an appeal for want of prosecution, or by consent, dismiss it, or allow it to be withdrawn and deal with costs arising therefrom.

Any interlocutory application in connection with the appeal may be disposed of by a single judge.

Where the appeal relates only to the amount of periodical payments, it may be heard and determined by a single judge, and in this case fewer copies of documents need be lodged; it may then also be heard in a divorce town.

Practice Directions: by a Practice Direction dated 11 May 1977, the appellant's solicitor is under a duty to certify whether there are other matrimonial proceedings pending between the same parties. Copies, in typescript, of documents put in at the hearing as exhibits must be lodged with the other documents. By a Practice Direction dated 10 July 1970, where a justices' clerk is served with a notice of appeal he should immediately forward to the chief clerk of the Contentious Department of the Family Division the exhibits which were handed in at the hearing and any welfare report which was considered.

(e) Bringing the appeal

The appeal is commenced by originating motion; which must state the grounds and the ambit of the appeal. The grounds must be paragraphed with particularity; vague words are not acceptable. The grounds may be amended, however, with the leave of the court hearing the appeal (O.55 r.6).

The notice of motion must state whether the appeal is against the whole or part only of the order complained of; and if part only, which part. The bringing of such an appeal does not operate as a stay of proceedings unless the court by which the appeal is to be heard so orders (see however the power of magistrates to suspend operation of an order made under DPMCA 1978; subject to that any order may be enforced in the normal way).

By RSC 1965 O.55 r.4, the persons to be served with the notice of motion of appeal are the justices' clerk; and any party to the proceedings who is directly affected by the appeal.

For the purposes of an appeal from magistrates in domestic proceedings, notice must be served and the appeal entered within six weeks after the date of the order, but this period may be extended with leave of the court.

Where an appeal is brought against a magistrates' decision in proceedings other than domestic proceedings, notice must be served and the appeal entered within 27 days after the date of the order. Service of notice of motion must comply with RSC 1965 OO.10 and 65.

The periods specified above are calculated from the date on which notice of the decision is given to the appellant by the court.

By O.65 r.5, unless the court having jurisdiction to determine the appeal otherwise directs, the hearing of the appeal shall not be sooner than 21 days after service of the notice of motion.

(f) Powers of court hearing appeal

In domestic cases, DPMCA 1978 s.29 provides that the High Court may make any order as necessary to give effect to its determination of the appeal; this includes any incidental or consequential order as appropriate, as well as provision to ante-date an order for payment so as to commence at the date of the application in the magistrates' court. Where on appeal an order or interim order for periodical payments is reduced or discharged, the court may order the person entitled to such payment to repay such sums as have been paid or remit arrears accrued.

Any order made on appeal shall be treated for enforcement purposes as an order made by a magistrates' court. Other powers of the appellate court are contained in O.56 r.7.

In cases other than domestic proceedings, the court may (RSC 1965 O.56 r.7):

(i) receive further evidence on questions of fact, and such evidence may be given in any manner the court thinks fit;

(ii) draw an inference of fact which might have been drawn in the lower court;

(iii) give any judgment or decision or make any order which ought to have been given or made by the magistrates' court, and make such further order as the case may require, or remit the matter with the opinion of the court for rehearing and determination;

(iv) in special circumstances, order that security shall be given for the costs of the appeal;

(v) allow the appeal, notwithstanding the grounds are merely a misdirection, or improper admission or rejection of evidence; unless a miscarriage of justice is apparent.

Legal aid to appeal (O.55): may be granted by The Law Society, not the courts, by means of a certificate under LA(G)R 1971 Regs. 3, 5 and 6 (see page 104).

8. Application to the High Court for judicial review

(a) Scope of judicial review jurisdiction

RSC 1965 O.53 contains the provisions and regulates the procedure for the exercise by the High Court of it supervisory jurisdiction over the proceedings and decisions of magistrates' courts. The judicial review procedure enables a person seeking to challenge an act or omission of a magistrates' court to apply to the High Court for one or any of the prerogative orders of *mandamus, prohibition* or *certiorari*. The procedure is for a review of proceedings and not strictly an appeal; the orders are discretionary and may be withheld if there has been undue delay in bringing the case forward. Where there was an appeal to a Crown Court (against a compensation order against an offender) judicial review was not appropriate: *R* v *Battle Justices ex parte Shepherd and Another* (1983).

Mandamus: an order of *mandamus* requires an act to be done, and may be made where an inferior court has failed to act or carry out its proper function. The order is made where there is a legal right to act but no other specified, convenient, or effective remedy is available. It may be issued where justices have refused to state a case in the belief that the appeal is frivolous (see page 120). Disobedience to an order is punishable by committal for contempt.

Prohibition: this remedy lies, *inter alia*, to restrain a magistrates' court from exceeding jurisdiction, and it may be issued before the court has made its final decision.

Certiorari: this order has the effect of removing proceedings from magistrates' courts to the High Court; and thus ensures that judgments, orders, convictions and other proceedings therein may be quashed. The order requires the records of the proceedings to be transmitted to the High Court to be quashed.

Judicial review proceedings are becoming very popular for alleging natural justice has been contravened. Whenever the statute or rules omit to deal with a situation, natural justice can fill the gap. "Justices who go on with the hearing of a charge against a defendant who is handicapped [in this case, totally deaf] take a very considerable risk of the hearing which they conduct being described as contrary to natural justice": *R* v *Kingston-upon-Thames Magistrates' Court ex parte Davey* (1985). The rules are silent on the question of whether a juvenile court should give a parent, in care proceedings, notice that it is considering making an order to prevent him representing the child (C&YPA 1969 s.32A). Court practice varies, and this problem is currently before the High Court.

(b) Two stage process for judicial review

Applications for judicial review are made in two stages; it is necessary to obtain the leave of the court (r.3) and only if and to the extent that leave is granted, will the court proceed to hear the substantive application.

Application for leave is made *ex parte* to a Divisional Court (or, in vacation, to a judge in chambers, with the right of making a fresh application to the Divisional Court after the vacation if refused) and must be supported by:

   (i)   a statement setting out the name and description of the applicant, the relief sought and the grounds on which it is sought;

   (ii) an affidavit filed before the application is made verifying the facts relied on.

Notice of the application must be given to the Crown Office not later than the day before the application is made, and copies of the statement and every affidavit must also be lodged. The statement may be amended as to grounds, relief sought, or otherwise with the leave of the court.

Only a person who has a sufficient interest in the matter to which the application relates may successfully apply for judicial review. This may be a direct and personal interest, or a general or public interest; the question will be one of fact and degree, and/or fact and law, and the relationship between the applicant and the matter in question.

The court granting leave may make any order as to costs and as to giving security as it thinks just.

Any application granted in respect of one of the prerogative orders shall, if the court so directs, operate as a stay of proceedings until determination of the application or other order.

(c) Mode of application for judicial review

When leave has been granted, the application is made, in criminal cases, by originating motion to a Divisional Court of the Queen's Bench Division (or to a judge in chambers in vacation); and, in civil cases, by motion in open court, or by originating summons in chambers.

The notice of motion or summons must be served on all persons directly affected; and where the relief sought is to compel a court to do any act in relation to court proceedings, or quash them or quash an order made therein, on the clerk of that court.

Unless the court granting leave directs otherwise, there must be at least 10 days between service of the notice of motion or summons, and the date of hearing, but the notice or summons must be entered for hearing within 14 days after the grant of leave. Copies thereof, together with statements, affidavits and exhibits, must be left for the use of the judge of the Divisional Court.

An affidavit giving the names and addresses and the places and dates of service on all persons who have been served with the notice of motion or summons must be filed before the notice or summons is entered for hearing. If any person has not been served who should have been, the affidavit must state the fact and reason therefor; the court may adjourn the hearing on terms to ensure service is effected.

Copies of the statement and affidavit in support of the application for leave must be served with the notice of motion or summons; and, except with leave of the court, no grounds shall be relied on or relief sought except as set out in the statement.

(d) Hearing of application

Any person who desires to be heard, and appears to be a proper person to be heard, may be heard in opposition to the application, notwithstanding that he has not been served with a notice of motion or the summons.

Where an order of *certiorari* is made the order shall direct that the proceedings be quashed on their removal to the Queen's Bench Division; and in addition remits the matter back to the magistrates' court to reconsider it and reach a decision in accordance with the finding of the court.

Where the relief sought is or includes an order of *certiorari* to quash proceedings, the application may not question any order, warrant, commitment, conviction or record, unless, before the hearing, the applicant has lodged a copy in the Crown Office and verified it by affidavit; or has accounted for his failure to do so to the satisfaction of the court.

(e) Legal aid

Similar provisions for applying for a legal aid certificate, again, to The Law Society, not the courts, apply to application for judicial review as to appeals to the High Court; see page 107.

Appendix 1

Forms

Contents

Forms LA/Rep/6A, LA/Rep/3B, LA/Rep/6A/1 LA/Rep/12, the Key Card and Legal Aid and Remuneration Summary are drafted by, and are reproduced with the permission of, The Law Society.

Appeals

1. Form of information

.... MAGISTRATES' COURT (Code)

THE INFORMATION of ....

of..

WHO STATES that ....

of..

on the ...... day of .... 19... at ....

....

did ....

CONTRARY TO Section/Regulation ....
Taken before me,

                              [Justice of the Peace for ....]
                              [Justices' Clerk   ]

LA/Rep/6A
GREEN FORM

THE LAW SOCIETY

 LEGAL AID
ENGLAND and WALES

SOLICITOR'S REPORT ON LEGAL ADVICE AND ASSISTANCE GIVEN UNDER
THE LEGAL AID ACT 1974

Key Card

PLEASE USE BLOCK CAPITALS

Surname	Forenames	Male/Female	AREA REF. No.
Address			

CAPITAL		CLIENT	£
TOTAL SAVINGS and OTHER CAPITAL		SPOUSE	£
		TOTAL	£

INCOME
State whether in receipt of Supplementary Benefit or Family Income Supplement.
YES/NO   If the answer is YES ignore the rest of this Section.

Total weekly Gross Income

Client	£
Spouse	£
TOTAL	£

Allowances and Deductions from Income

Income tax	£
National Health Contributions, etc.	£
Spouse	£

Dependent children and/or other dependants	Number	
Under 5		£
5 but under 11		£
11 „ „ 13		£
13 „ „ 16		£
16 „ „ 18		£
18 and over		£

LESS TOTAL DEDUCTIONS	➤	£
TOTAL WEEKLY DISPOSABLE INCOME		£

NOTE TO SOLICITORS
With effect from 1st April 1977

Where advice and assistance are being given in respect of divorce or judicial separation proceedings and the work to be carried out includes the preparation of a petition, the solicitor will be entitled to ask for his claim for Costs and Disbursements to be assessed up to an amount referred to in a general authority given by the Area Committee to exceed the prescribed basic sum in such cases.

TO BE COMPLETED AND SIGNED BY CLIENT

I am over the compulsory school-leaving age.

I have/have not previously received help from a solicitor about this matter under the Legal Aid and Advice Schemes.

I am liable to pay a contribution not exceeding .. .. | £ |

I understand that any money or property which is recovered or preserved for me may be subject to a deduction if my contribution (if any) is less than my Solicitor's charges.

The information on this page is to the best of my knowledge correct and complete. I understand that dishonesty in providing such information may lead to a prosecution.

Date........................   Signature..

THE LAW SOCIETY

GREEN FORM KEY CARD
(No. 17)
Effective from 12th March 1986

 Green Form

N.B. The green form (LA/Rep/6A) should not be used for advice to suspects at police stations from 1st January 1986. Such cases will be covered by forms LA/Rep/12 and LA/Acc 10 which were supplied to the profession during December 1985.

CAPITAL means the amount or value of every resource of a capital nature
In computing Disposable Capital disregard
(i) the value of the main or only dwelling house in which the client resides, and
(ii) the value of household furniture and effects, articles of personal clothing and tools or implements of the client's trade, and
(iii) the subject matter of the advice and assistance.

Maximum Disposable Capital for Financial Eligibility (dependant=spouse, child or relative)

Advice and Assistance	Assistance by way of representation
£ 800 – client with no dependants	£3000 – client with no dependants
£1000 – client with 1 dependant	£3200 – client with 1 dependant
£1120 – client with 2 dependants	£3320 – client with 2 dependants
Add £60 for each additional dependant	

The capital and weekly income of both husband and wife must be taken into account, unless:
(a) they have a contrary interest;
(b) they live apart; or
(c) it is inequitable or impracticable to aggregate their means.
If a housewife living with her husband is seeking advice in connection with a matter in which he has a contrary interest, the money which she receives from him for normal household expenses should not be included as part of her own separate income.

INCOME means the total income from all sources which the client received or became entitled to during or in respect of the seven days up to and including the date of this application.

Note – a client in receipt of supplementary benefit or family income supplement is entitled to advice and assistance without contribution provided that his disposable capital is within the limits set out in **A** above.

In computing Disposable Income deduct:-
(i) Income Tax

(ii) Payments under the Social Security Acts 1975-80

(iii) £28.75 in respect of either husband or wife (if living together) whether or not their means are aggregated. Where they are separated or divorced, the allowance will be the actual maintenance paid by the client in respect of the previous 7 days.

These deductions also apply to the spouse's income if there is aggregation.

(iv) £12.65 for each dependent child or dependent relative of the household under 11 years of age
£18.90 for each dependent child or dependent relative of the household of 11 but under 16 years of age
£22.75 for each dependent child or dependent relative of the household of 16 and 17 years of age
£29.50 for each dependent child or dependent relative of the household of 18 years of age or over

There is no deduction in relation to a foster child.

Client's Contributions

Disposable Income	Maximum Contribution	Disposable Income	Maximum Contribution
Not exceeding £54 a week	nil	Not exceeding £83 a week	£29
,, £62 ,,	£5	,, £87 ,,	£34
,, £67 ,,	£11	,, £91 ,,	£38
,, £71 ,,	£16	,, £95 ,,	£42
,, £75 ,,	£21	,, £99 ,,	£47
,, £79 ,,	£25	,, £104 ,,	£52
		,, £108 ,,	£57
		,, £114 ,,	£62

Where the initial green form limit is £50 client's contribution in excess of this amount can only be called for if a financial extension has been obtained from the general committee.

 Note The green form must be signed by the client at the initial interview as soon as his eligibility has been determined except in the case of an authorised postal application.

CLAIM FOR PAYMENT TO ACCOMPANY FORM LA/ACC/8B

Name of Client

Where appropriate did the Court give approval to assistance under Section 2 (4) of the Legal Aid Act 1974 ? Yes/No.

Has a Legal Aid Order been made ? Yes/No.

If so, give date

PLEASE ATTACH ANY AUTHORITIES GIVEN BY THE AREA COMMITTEE

TICK THE APPROPRIATE LETTER TO INDICATE THE NATURE OF THE PROBLEM

A. Divorce or judicial separation (see note on page 1)

B. Other family matters (Specify in Summary)

C. Crime

D. Landlord/tenant/housing

E. H.P. and Debt

F. Employment

G. Accident/injuries

H. Welfare benefits/tribunals

J. Immigration/Nationality

K. Consumer problems

L. Other matters (Specify in Summary)

Has any money or property been recovered? If so, give details.

No. of letters written	
No. of telephone calls Made Received	
Time otherwise spent: Specify in Summary	

Summary of work done :

Has a legal aid certificate or order been granted? Yes/No.

If not, is one being applied for ? Yes/No.

Certificate or Order No. if appropriate :

PARTICULARS OF COSTS

£

1. Profit costs

2. Disbursements (including Counsel's fees)

3. Add VAT as appropriate

TOTAL CLAIM

4. Deduct maximum contribution (if any)

NET CLAIM

Details of disbursements :—

Counsel's fees (if any)

Other disbursements (listed)

£

Have you previously made a claim for legal advice and assistance for your client in respect of divorce or judicial separation proceedings or matters connected therewith. YES/NO If Yes, how much was allowed £

Signed Solicitor Date Solicitor's ref.

Firm name (in full)

Address

Date

NOTICE OF PROVISIONAL ASSESSMENT

The Area Committee have assessed your costs in this matter as set out below. In view of the fact that the sum assessed is less than that claimed, you may make written representations to the Committee in support of your claim as originally submitted or on any item in it, if you wish. These representations must be received within 14 days of the date hereof. I have deleted this matter from the consolidated claim form LA/ACC/8B with which it was sent and I should be obliged if you would do the same. If you accept the provisional assessment, please include this matter on your next consolidated claim form as assessed below AND RE-SUBMIT THIS FORM WITH IT.

Area Secretary.

£

1. Profit costs

2. Disbursements

3. Add VAT as appropriate

TOTAL CLAIM

4. Deduct maximum contribution (if any)

NET CLAIM

NOTE.—You are advised to keep a copy of this page because if in the same matter your client obtains a L.A. Certificate or Order, you may on taxation of your costs and disbursements be required to produce to the Taxing Officer a copy of this form indicating work done and quantum of payment. You may also require a copy of this page if after submitting your claim for payment you apply to the Area Committee for a financial extension to enable you to give further advice and assistance to your Client.

APRIL 1977

GREEN FORM KEY CARD (No. 17)
EXPLANATORY NOTES

1. General

Your attention is particularly drawn to the *Legal Advice and Assistance Regulations (No. 2) 1980* ("the regulations") *pp. 107-123 Legal Aid Handbook 1984* and the *Notes for Guidance on Advice and Assistance* issued by the Council of The Law Society which appear in the *Handbook pp. 199-209.*

2. Financial Eligibility

(a) The responsibility for determining eligibility is placed upon the solicitor *(reg. 7).*

(b) *Schedule 2* of the regulations sets out the method of assessment of resources of the client. The only deductions and allowances which can be made are those referred to in *schedule 2.* Built-in deductions have already been made for miscellaneous expenditure such as rent, mortgage repayments and hire-purchase repayments etc.

(c) When considering a client's means it may be useful to have the following points in mind –

(i) If part of the main dwelling is let and the client lives in the remaining part, although the capital value of the main dwelling house should be left out of account in computing capital, the rent should be included in computing income.

(ii) Capital means the amount or value of every resource of a capital nature so that capital derived from a bank loan or borrowing facilities should be taken into account.

(iii) There is no power to disregard income in self-employed cases merely because the client may have incurred unspecified expenses at an earlier date.

(iv) A cohabitee cannot be included within the definitions of a spouse or dependant. No allowances can therefore be made in respect of a cohabitee nor can his/her income be aggregated with that of the client seeking advice or assistance.

(v) Income means the total income from all sources which the client received or became entitled to during or in respect of the seven days up to and including the date of application. It will include child benefit.

(vi) Fostering allowances received in respect of fostered children should not be taken into account in assessing the financial eligibility of the client.

3. Solicitor and Client relationship

(a) A solicitor for reasonable cause may either refuse to accept an application for legal advice and assistance or having accepted it, decline to give advice and assistance without giving reasons to the client. He may however be required to give reasons to the general committee.

(b) Once financial eligibility has been established, a client should be told of the amount of the contribution due (if any), and arrangements should be made for payment either outright or by instalments. Any contribution paid should be retained on client's account until the matter for which advice and assistance has been given has been concluded.

(c) When the contribution exceeds the costs payable and VAT, the excess should be returned to the client.

4. Remuneration

(a) No VAT is payable on the client's contribution but VAT is of course, payable upon the solicitors costs whether paid out of the legal aid fund or from the contribution paid by the client.

(b) The initial financial limit of expenditure (at present £50, or in the case of an undefended divorce or judicial separation petition case £90) is exclusive of VAT as is any financial extention granted.

(c) The financial limit of £90 in undefended divorce or judicial separation cases is only applicable where a petition has been drafted. It need not however have been filed.

(d) The legal aid fund is only responsible for paying to solicitor and counsel such of their costs as are not covered by the client's contribution (if any) party and party costs awarded and the charge which arises in the solicitors favour on any property recovered or preserved. *Schedule 5* of the regulations sets out the circumstances when the charge does not apply. Application may be made to the area committee for authority not to enforce the charge where (a) it would cause grave hardship or distress to the client, or (b) it could be enforced only with unreasonable difficulty – *(reg 26.)*

5. Authorities

A solicitor may not take steps in court proceedings unless either approval is given by the general committee for assistance by way of representation in a magistrates' court or the court has made a request under *reg 19* of the regulations. It should be noted that the financial limit prescribed by *section 3(2) of the Legal Aid Act 1974* (at present £50) cannot be exceeded when a request has been made under *reg 19* and the solicitor has represented the client.

(a) The authority of the general committee is required before accepting an application from a child *(reg 8(1)),* a person on behalf of a child or patient, such person not falling with the categories referred to in reg 8(2)(a) (b) or (c) *(reg 8(2)(d)),* a person residing outside England and Wales *(reg 9)* and a person who has already received advice and assistance from another solicitor on the same matter *(reg 10).*

(b) Approval of the general committee is required for assistance by way of representation *(reg 17(1)).* Even if approval is given the prior permission of the general committee is required to obtain a report, or opinion of an expert to tender expert evidence and to perform an act which is either unusual in its nature or involves unusually large expenditure *(reg 17(4).)* Thus the prior permission of the general committee would be required before obtaining a blood test in affiliation proceedings.

MARCH 1986

3. Application for Legal Aid (Legal Aid Act 1974, s. 28; Legal Aid in Criminal Proceedings (General) Regulations)

Application for Legal Aid
PLEASE USE BLOCK CAPITALS

1. Name ....
   Address ....
   .... Date of Birth ....
2. I apply for legal aid at the Crown/Magistrates'/Juvenile Court sitting
   at...
   My case is due to be heard on ....
   at .... a.m./p.m.
3. Is any other person charged with you in these proceedings?   YES/NO
4. The solicitor I wish to act for me is (*state name and address*).......
   ....
5. Describe shortly what it is you are accused of doing, eg. "stealing £50
   from my employer", "kicking a door causing £50 damage".
   ....

I understand that I (or my parents if I am under 16) may be required by the
Supplementary Benefits Commission to supply further information about
my means. I also understand that the court may order me to make a
contribution to the costs of legal aid or to pay the whole costs if it considers
that my means enable me to do so and, if I am under 16, may make a similar
order with respect to my parents.

Signed .... Dated ....

Reasons for wanting Legal Aid
When deciding whether to grant you legal aid, the court will need to know
the reasons why it is in the interests of justice for you to be represented. You
are therefore *requested* to complete the remainder of this form to avoid the
possibility of legal aid being refused because the court does not have
sufficient information about the case. *If you need help in completing the
form and especially if you have previous convictions, you should see a
solicitor.* He may be able to advise you free of charge or at a reduced fee.
If you plead *not guilty*, the information in this form will not be made known
to the magistrates who try your case, unless they convict you. If you are
acquitted the financial information will be given to them.

6. I am in real danger of a custodial sentence because (*give brief reasons*):
   ....
7. If you were convicted of the present charge, would you be in breach of
   any court order, ie suspended sentence of imprisonment, conditional
   discharge, probation, community service; or are you subject to a
   deferred sentence? (*give brief details so far as you are able including the
   date(s) on which the sentence(s) was/were imposed*):
   ....
   ....

8. I am in real danger of losing my livelihood or suffering serious damage to my reputation because (*give brief reasons*):

....
....

9. A substantial question of law is involved (*give brief details*):

....

10. I shall be unable to follow the proceedings because:
    (a) My knowledge of English is inadequate   YES/NO
    (b) I suffer from a disability, namely ....

....

11. Witnesses have to be traced and interviewed on my behalf (*state circumstances*):

....
....

12. The case involves expert cross-examination of a prosecution witness (*give brief details*):

....

13. The case is a very complex one, for example, mistaken identity (*explain briefly*):

....

14. Any other reason (*give full particulars*):

....
....

4. Statement of Means by Applicant or Appropriate Contributor for Legal Aid Purposes
(General Reg. 4(1))

To apply for criminal legal aid you must complete this form. If you are not yet sixteen, then your mother or father may also be asked to complete one. If you have applied for legal aid for your child, and your child is sixteen years old or over, then **you** do not need to fill in this form. **Your child** should complete it, giving details of his or her **own income**.

This information is needed before legal aid can be granted, so to avoid any delay in your application being considered, please complete this form as fully and as carefully as possible.

SECTION 1 — PERSONAL DETAILS

1. Full name (*block letters please*) ....
2. Date of birth ....
3. Home address ....
....
4. Marital status (*please tick one box*)
   - ☐ single   ☐ divorced
   - ☐ married   ☐ widow(er)
   - ☐ married but separated

135

5. Occupation (*state 'unemployed' if appropriate*)
   List here **all** your jobs, including any part-time work and your employer's name and address. (If you have more than one job, give the name and address of each employer; if self-employed state 'self').
   ....
   ....

SECTION 2 — PERSONAL DETAILS (DEPENDENT CHILD)

If legal aid is being sought for a dependent child, and he or she is not yet sixteen, please answer the following questions about him or her.

1. Full name (*block letters please*) ....
2. Date of birth ....
3. Home address (*if different from yours*) ....
   ....
4. Your relationship to him or her (*e.g. father*) ....

SECTION 3 — FINANCIAL DETAILS

Part A — Income
Please give below details of your net income (*i.e. after the deduction of tax and national insurance*) from all sources for the three months immediately before this form is completed. If you are married and living with your wife or husband, then you have to provide details of his or her income as well. The court may ask you to provide proof of the information you give in this form.

Your contribution, if any, will be assessed and collected on a **weekly** basis, so if you are paid monthly, please give **weekly** figures.

1. Do you receive Supplementary Benefit?

   ☐ Yes— *You do not need to complete the rest of this form, simply turn to the declaration section and sign it.*

   ☐ No— *Please go on to question two.*

2. Do you receive Family Income Supplement?

   ☐ Yes— *There is no need to complete any more of Part A, so please turn to Part B — Capital and Savings.*

   ☐ No— *Please go on to question three.*

3. Please give details of your INCOME in the table below.

Description of INCOME	Amount		Remarks
	Your income	Income of husband/wife	
(a) Weekly earnings or salary, including overtime, commission or bonuses. (Please give net figures). Please attach with this form your last six wage slips. If you do not have that many, please attach as many as you can.			
(b) If your earnings change from week to week, give the amounts for the last 13 weeks. (If you do not have this information, please give the amounts for as many weeks as you can, and at least the last 6 weeks. You should if possible attach wage slips).			
(c) Income from any part-time job not included at (a) above. (Please give gross and net figures).			
(d) Income from state benefits — e.g. family allowance (*please specify below here*).			
(e) Gross income from sub-letting house, rooms, etc.			
(f) Any other income (*please give details below here*).			
(g) If in a business of your own, please attach the most recent accounts available.			

IMPORTANT: If the information you have given in the table above is going to change soon, please give details of the change in section 5 of this form.

Part B — Capital and Savings
Please give details of **all** your capital and savings. If you are married and living with your husband or wife, also give details of his or her capital and savings. You should give particulars of savings with the National Savings Bank or with other banks. National Savings Certificates, cash stocks and shares or any other investments. Please also give details of any property you own, such as houses or flats apart from the house or flat in which you live.

1. Please give details of your *CAPITAL and SAVINGS* in the table below.

Description of CAPITAL and SAVINGS	Amount		Remarks
	You	Husband/Wife	
(a) Do you own house property (apart from your main or only dwelling)? (*Answer YES or NO*)	YES/NO	YES/NO	
(b) if YES state: (i) The value (*i.e. the approximate selling price*) (ii) The amount of any outstanding mortgage.			
(c) Give details of your savings. (*State saving Institution below here*)			
Give details of any articles of value that you own (*e.g. jewellery, furs, paintings*) with their approximate value.			

SECTION 4 — ALLOWANCES AND DEDUCTIONS

In assessing your means for legal aid purposes, the court will make allowances for the cost of supporting your husband or wife, children and any other dependent relatives, and also for your accommodation costs and travelling expenses. If there are any other expenses which you think the court should make allowance for, please give details at question 4 below.

1. Please give the NUMBER of dependants who are *LIVING WITH YOU*.

Husband or wife	Children 18 and over	Children 16 and 17	Children 11 to 15	Children under 11	Other *(specify below)*

2. If you pay maintenance to a dependant who does not live with you, please give details of the amounts you pay to support them.

Age of dependant	Your relationship to him or her	Amount you pay per week

3. You may claim for the HOUSING EXPENSES of you and your wife or husband. Please give the amounts you pay each week. If you own more than one house, only give details connected with the house in which you live. If you are paying the housing expenses of (a) dependant(s) who do(es) not live with you, please give both amounts.

Description of payment	Amount per week	Amount per week for dependant(s)
Rent		
Mortgage repayment		
Ground rent		
Service charge		
Rates		
Board and lodging		
Bed and breakfast		

4. The TRAVELLING EXPENSES of you and your husband or wife may be taken into account. You may claim for the actual amounts that you and your husband or wife spend per week travelling to and from your place(s) of employment.

	You	Your husband or wife
Amount spent		

5. Please give details of any OTHER EXPENSES which you think the court should know about.

Description of expenditure	Amount spent per week

6. Allowance for contributions in respect of LEGAL ADVICE AND ASSISTANCE under the "green form" scheme.
   You may already have been given some advice and assistance by a solicitor under the "green form" scheme, and you may have paid, or been asked to pay, a contribution towards that advice. If this is the case, then the amount of your legal aid contribution will be reduced by the amount of "green form" contribution you have paid.

Name and address of the solicitor who gave the advice and assistance	Amount of contribution paid (or to be paid)

SECTION 5 — FURTHER INFORMATION

This part of the form is set aside for you to give any financial information that you think the court should have when deciding upon your application for legal aid. You may also use this part of the form to tell the court of any future changes in circumstance that might alter your financial position.

SECTION 6 — DECLARATION

Anyone who has knowingly or recklessly made a statement which is false in any way, or has knowingly withheld information is liable to be prosecuted and, if convicted, to either imprisonment for a term not exceeding four months, or to a fine or both. After your application has been considered by the court, you may be asked to give further information or to clarify information that you have already given. In particular you may be required to provide documentary proof of the information you have given (e.g. wage slips, rent books, etc.)

I declare that to the best of my knowledge and belief, I have given a complete and correct statement of my income, savings and capital (and that of my husband or wife)* (and that of my child)**.

Date . . . . Signed . . . .

  * Delete if you are not living with your husband or wife, or if you are single.
** Delete if legal aid is not sought for your child.

LA/Rep/3B

The Law Society

No covering letter necessary — explanatory notes on reverse

Legal Aid in Criminal Proceedings (Fees and Expenses) Regulations 1968 (as amended)

A		Serial Number		SP		FOR OFFICIAL USE ONLY

Number of Defendants if more than one

Initials and Surname of Main Defendant

If you acted for more than one legally aided defendant, list their names overleaf and enter the total number in the right hand box

1. Name of court and date of charge
2. Brief description of charge(s)

1.
2.

Date

3. Type of hearing

4. Plea — Where case tried
5. Result of trial or hearing
6. Was your client ordered to pay a contribution? If so, amount
7. Was Counsel assigned?
8. If not, was Counsel instructed?

3. * Summary trial/Preliminary hearing (Quote section)
4. * Guilty/Not Guilty
5. * Guilty/Not Guilty/Committed
6. * No/Yes. Amount £

7. * Yes/No
8. * Yes/No
   * Delete as necessary

Summary of all work done

(If there is insufficient space to enable you to provide the details required to justify your charges, continue on a separate sheet)

Personal attendances (taking statements, etc.)				Correspondence & telephone calls		Attendance at court (Apportion travelling time if more than one case)		
Client		Other persons				Time taken		
Date	Time taken	Date	Time taken	No. of letters written		Date	Travelling	Waiting	Hearing
				No. of telephone calls					

Special features (if any) ....

....

....

(Use separate letter if appropriate)

Claims for Costs

If you have advised your client in connection with this matter under a GREEN FORM which you had already submitted for assessment, please give the date of the relevant form LA/ACC/8B. If you have not yet submitted a GREEN FORM for assessment and intend to do so, please attach it together with a form LA/ACC/8B to this form. Date of LA/ACC/8B

	Solicitor's costs	Disbursements	Counsel's fees (Total including VAT as shown on fee note)
Basic fee		As Listed Overleaf	
Adjournment fee(s)			
Additional Defendants			
Work on appeal			
Total Fees			
Plus VAT %			
Totals	£	£	£

Do you wish to make any comment on the fee claimed by Counsel. (See explanatory Note No. 6)

Solicitor's reference ....

Signed .... Solicitor Date........................

Firm name (in full) ....

Address ....

Counsel's Name & Address ....

B		Control		For official use only Sol. A/c No.		Coun. A/c		Counsel Assigned

Authorised for Payment

Date .... Signed ....

Explanatory Notes

1. You have received a set of three copies of this form. When completed you should send the first and second copies to the appropriate Area Secretary. The third copy should be retained by you to identify payment.

2. You should set out overleaf the fees to which you consider you are entitled for work actually done by you and counsel where instructed and forward the following documents:-

    (a) Original Legal Aid Order;

    (b) Your client's proof of evidence and copies of statements by witnesses;

    (c) Counsel's endorsed brief (in those cases where counsel has been instructed, whether assigned or not);

    (d) Vouchers or receipts for out-of-pocket expenses incurred;

    (e) Where Counsel is employed, his case memorandum and completed fee note.

The Area Committee may call for the production of your complete file of papers.

3. If you consider that any maximum fee prescribed in the schedule to The Legal Aid in Criminal Proceedings (Fees and Expenses) Regulations 1968 as amended would not provide fair remuneration you should insert the amounts regarded as justified and set out the relevant circumstances under the heading "Special Features". It will greatly assist if details of the work done under the Legal Aid Order can be confined to the space provided. This would prove possible in most cases. The Area Committee only require an adequate summary sufficient to enable them to make a fair and reasonable assessment.

4. The fees which may be paid to a solicitor are prescribed by the Legal Aid in Criminal Proceedings (Fees and Expenses) Regulations 1968 as amended.

5. A Solicitor may instruct Counsel in any case in which Counsel is not assigned if he wishes to do so, but if he does, the Area Committee will first assess the maximum fee allowable under the regulations as if the case had been conducted by the Solicitor alone and thereafter assess fair remuneration for work actually and reasonably done by Counsel and fair remuneration for work actually and reasonably done by the Solicitor. If the maximum fee is insufficient to pay fair remuneration to both, the Area Committee will exercise its discretion and apportion the maximum fee payable having regard to all the relevant circumstances.

6. If you wish to make any comment on the fee claimed by Counsel you should write a separate letter which should be attached to this form. Before the costs are assessed by the Area Committee a copy of your letter will be submitted to Counsel to enable him to consider your representations.

7. Adjournment fees may only be claimed when the case was actually opened in a previous hearing and was adjourned part heard.

8. If your client was called upon to pay a contribution in respect of the legal aid provided under the Legal Aid Order, the amount of the costs allowed to you will be notified by the Area Committee to the Clerk to the Justices to enable him to consider whether any repayment of contribution can be made.

Names of additional defendants (if any)
in receipt of legal aid.

Detailed List of Disbursements

	£	p
Travelling expenses (if car, state mileage)		
Other expenses (list)		
VAT (as appropriate)		
Total		

N.B. Vouchers, loss of wages certificates, statements and other documents likely to be needed to enable a fair and reasonable assessment to be made should be forwarded.

LA/Rep/6A/1

THE LAW SOCIETY
Legal Aid Acts 1974 and 1979

ENGLAND and WALES

Application for Assistance by way of Representation

Area Ref. No.

PLEASE USE BLOCK CAPITALS

Client's surname .... Forenames .... Mr., Mrs. or M

Address ....

....

....

Occupation .... Date of birth ....

**I am acting for my client
under a Green Form dated** ....

**Date of hearing
(if known)** ....

I have assessed my client's contribution as £ ....

NB. The Legal Aid Certificate procedure is still available for Magistrates Court proceedings if the clients means are in excess of the Green For eligibility limits but within those of Legal Aid.

(Tick box as applicable)

**My client requires assistance
by way of representation for**

TAKING ☐

DEFENDING ☐

proceedings relating to:-

1. Maintenance or financial provision ☐

2. Custody, access, maintenance or financial provision for child ☐

3. A protection or exclusion order ☐

4. Affiliation ☐

5. Revocation or variation of a maintenance or financial provision order ☐

6. Enforcement of a maintenance order made by the Court outside the United Kingdom ☐

7. An opposed application for an Adoption Order by any party to the proceedings ☐

8. The assumption by a local authority of parental rights over a child in care ☐

9. Compelling a local authority to bring a child or young person before a Court as being in need of care, protection or control ☐

10. The recovery of the cost of assistance or benefit from a person liable for maintenance ☐

Signed .... Solicitor Dated .... Solictor's reference ....

Firm name (in full) ....

Address ....

....

....Tel. no. ....

For official use only

GRANTED/REFUSED

Conditions and limitations (if any)

Signed ....

Area Secretary No.

144

The following information should be supplied as appropriate

Full name and address of opponent	Names and ages of children
Occupation Date of birth	

Date of Marriage .... Date last lived together ....

STATEMENT OF CASE

Please set out below statement in support of application including details if appropriate of opponents financial resources (if known) and corroborative evidence in support. If the application relates to proceedings before a Mental Health Review Tribunal, any relevant documents should be supplied.

....
....
....
....
....
....
....
....
....
....
....
....
....
....
....
....
....
....
....
....
....
....
....

I authorise The Law Society to request the Clerk to the Justices to enforce any order for costs made in my favour in the proceedings for which approval may be given or to write off such costs if he considers they are irrecoverable or only recoverable at unjustified expense.

Signed by Client ....

LA/REP/12

Advice at Police Stations Report

The Legal Advice and Assistance at Police Stations (Remuneration) Regulations 1985

This form should be completed whether you acted as own solicitor or 24-hour duty solicitor.
Please complete sections 1, 2, 3 and 5 of this form. Complete section 4 only if you represented a client where the police made an application for a warrant of further detention or for the extension of such a warrant.
You should retain the first copy; the remaining copy should be sent to your legal aid area office.
If you advised more than one client in connection with the same incident please complete a separate LA/Rep/12 form for each client.

SECTION 1   Details of client receiving advice and assistance

Client's Surname   [   ]   Forenames   [   ]

Client's Address   [   ]

[   ]

SECTION 2

I was instructed as   own solicitor / 24-hour duty solicitor / both   (delete as appropriate)

Solicitor's Name   [   ]

Firm's Name   [   ]

Firm's Address   [   ]

[   ]   **office telephone**   (STD)

Police station where client located   [   ]

Date of first attendance   [   ]

Did you   (i)   advise and assist a client who had not been arrested or a client arrested in connection with a "non-arrestable" offence?   YES/NO

     (ii)   advise and assist an arrested client in connection with an arrestable offence?   YES/NO

        State nature of offence (if more than one, state the most serious)

        [   ]

     (iii)   advise and assist a Services person being investigated by the Services police?   YES/NO

If the matter upon which advice and assistance has been given relates to an arrestable offence, please explain why it was in the interests of justice to exceed the costs limit

[   ]

[   ]

Has the client previously received advice and assistance in respect of this matter?   YES/NO

If yes, please state the name of the solicitor and firm who previously gave advice and assistance.

[   ]

[   ]

COPY FOR SOLICITOR

SECTION 3

Work done as own solicitor
Attendance at police station

Time spent at police station from ☐ am/pm
to ☐ am/pm

Minutes spent travelling ☐

Minutes spent at police station waiting ☐

Minutes spent at police station advising and assisting client ☐

Total amount claimed for travel and at police station £ ☐ (A)

Telephone calls

Advising and assisting over telephone

number of calls ☐
minutes spent ☐

Routine telephone calls

number of calls ☐
minutes spent ☐

Total amount claimed for telephone calls £ ☐ (B)

Travel expenses £ ☐

Mileage ☐

Disbursements £ ☐

Details of disbursements ☐

Total amount claimed for travel expenses and disbursements £ ☐ (D)

Work done as 24-hour duty solicitor
Attendance at police station

Time spent at police station from ☐ am/pm
to ☐ am/pm

Minutes spent travelling ☐

Minutes spent waiting ☐

Minutes spent at police station ☐

Total amount claimed for travel and at police station £ ☐ (A)

Telephone calls

Advising and assisting over telephone

number of calls ☐
minutes spent ☐

Routine telephone calls

number of calls ☐
minutes spent ☐

Total amount claimed for telephone calls £ ☐ (B)

Travel expenses £ ☐

Mileage ☐

Disbursement £ ☐

Details of disbursements ☐

Total amount claimed for travel expenses and disbursements £ ☐ (D)

SECTION 4

To be completed only if you represented a client on an application for a warrant of further detention or an extension of such a warrant.

Total time spent from ☐ am/pm
to ☐ am/pm.

Travel time

Minutes spent travelling ☐

Total amount claimed for travelling £ ☐

Personal attendance

Minutes spent in attendance ☐

Total amount claimed for attendance £ ☐

Preparation

Minutes spent in preparation ☐

Total amount claimed for preparation £ ☐

Advocacy

Minutes spent in waiting ☐

Minutes spent in advocacy ☐

Total amount claimed for waiting and advocacy £ ☐

Letters and telephone calls

Letters written ☐

Telephone calls ☐

Total amount claimed for letters and telephone calls £ ☐

Total amount claimed for travel time, attendance, preparation, advocacy, letters and telephone calls £ ☐ (C)

Travel expenses £ ☐

Mileage ☐

Disbursements £ ☐

Details of disbursements ☐

Total amount claimed for travel expenses and disbursements £ ☐ (D)

SECTION 5

Profit Costs (A) + (B) (C) £ ☐
Disbursements (D) £ ☐
Add VAT as appropriate £ ☐
TOTAL £ ☐

Signed ☐
Date ☐
Solicitor's Ref ☐
Account No ☐

147

Legal Aid and Remuneration Summary
Legal Advice and Assistance at Police Stations

	Solicitor of choice	Duty Solicitor
Legal Aid Means Test	None	None
Legal Aid Contribution	None	None
Costs Limit		
Non-arrestable offence or volunteer	£50—unextendable	£50—unextendable
Arrestable offence	£90—retrospectively extendable by Area Office	£90—retrospectively extendable by Area Office
Solicitor's Hourly Rate		
Non-arrestable offence or volunteer	Standard green form rate *ie*, £17 travel and waiting £27 attendance. No enhanced rate for work done during unsocial hours*	£27 for attendance, travel and waiting. No enhanced rate for work done during unsocial hours*
Arrestable offence	As above	Enhanced rate of 1/3 over standard rate including travel for work done during unsocial hours*
Telephone Calls	£10 for each call where advice and assistance is given over the telephone. £1 for each other call	£10 for each call where advice and assistance is given over the telephone. £1 for each other call
Stand-by Payment	Not applicable	Stand-by payment of £2.50 per hour up to a maximum of £60 per 24-hour period. Duty solicitor must be on a rota, *ie*, not deployed under a panel arrangement. Offset to a maximum of 50% against any payment received for work done.
Hotel Expenses	Not applicable	Hotel expenses 'actually and reasonably incurred' will be paid if supported by receipts.

	Solicitor of choice	Duty Solicitor
ABWOR for Pre-charge Hearing	£27 preparation, £17 travel and waiting, £33 advocacy. No enhanced rate for work during unsocial hours*. £2.15 per item for letters and telephone calls.	£27 preparation, £17 travel and waiting, £33 advocacy, £2.15 per item for letters and telephone calls. For work done during unsocial hours* the rates are: £36 preparation, £23 travel and waiting, £44 advocacy. £2.75 per item for letters and telephone calls.

*'unsocial hours' means between 6 pm and 9 am on any weekday and any time on a Saturday, Sunday or bank holiday.

8. Complaint for order under Section 2 (DPMC Act 1978 ss.2, 30(2)) (Rule 3(1))

.... MAGISTRATES' COURT (Code)

Date: ....

Respondent: ....

Address: ....

The Application of: ....

Address: ....

Telephone No. ....

who applies for an order under Section 2 of the Domestic Proceedings and Magistrates' Courts Act 1978 on the ground[s] that the Respondent:

[(a) has failed to provide reasonable maintenance for the Applicant.]

[(b) has failed to provide, or to make a proper contribution towards, reasonable maintenance for any child of the family.]

[(c) has behaved in such a way that the Applicant cannot reasonably be expected to live with the Respondent.]

[(d) has deserted the Applicant.]

If ground (c) is alleged indicate briefly below the circumstances alleged to support that ground.

[Some courts require details of children]

Taken before me

Justice of the Peace
Justices' Clerk

149

9. Complaint for Order under Section 6 (DPMC Act 1978 ss.6, 30(2)) (Rule 4(1))

.... MAGISTRATES' COURT (Code)

Date: ....

Respondent:..

Address: ....

The Application of: ....

Address: ....

Telephone No..

who applies for an Order for financial provision under Section 6 of the Domestic Proceedings and Magistrates' Courts Act 1978 on the ground that the Respondent has agreed to:

[the making of periodical payments to the Applicant to the amount of £ .... per .... for a term of .... beginning on ....]

[the payment of a lump sum to the applicant to the amount of £ ....]

[the making of periodical payments to .... (being a child of the family)/the Applicant for the benefit of .... (being a child of the family) to the amount of £........... per .... for a term of .... beginning on ....]

[the payment of a lump sum to.............................. (being a child of the family/the Applicant for the benefit of .... (being a child of the family) to the amount of £ ....]

Taken before me

Justice of the Peace
Justices' Clerk

10. Consent to Order under Section 6 (DPMC Act 1978, S.6(8)) (Rule 4(3))

Concerning the application made by ....

(*applicant's name*) to be heard on .... (*Date*)

*I, ... (*full name*), hereby consent to the making of an Order for financial provision under Section 6 of the Domestic Proceedings and Magistrates' Courts Act 1978 in the terms set out in the

Summons dated...................... which I have received.

OR (*If you are completing this form before a Summons is issued*)

*I, ... (*full name*), hereby consent to the making of an Order for financial provision under Section 6 of the Domestic Proceedings and Magistrates' Courts Act 1978 in the following terms:

[the making of periodical payments to the Applicant to the amount of

£ .... per .... for a term of ....
beginning on ....]
[the payment of a lump sum to the Applicant to the amount of £ ....
(*Specify conditions of payment*)

[the making of periodical payments to ....]
(being a child of the family)/the Applicant for the benefit of ....
(being a child of the family) to the amount of £........ per........ for
a term of .... beginning on ....]
[the payment of a lump sum to .... (being a
child of the family)/the Applicant for the benefit of ....
.... (being a child of the family) to the amount of £ .... (*Specify
conditions of payment*)

*Delete whichever is inappropriate   ]

I, ... (*full name*), declare that my financial
resources are as follows:

Means

1. (*If you work for an employer*)
   Usual pay (including overtime and
   bonuses)
   Gross (before deductions)   £ .... per
                                          week/month/year
   Net (after deductions)   £ .... per
                                          week/month/year

2. (*If you are self-employed*)
   Gross profits over last twelve months £ ....
   Outgoings from the business in the
   last twelve months   £ ....
   Income tax demand for last year   £ ....

3. Amount received in State benefits   £ .... per week

4. Any other income (state source)   £ .... per
                                          week/month/year

5. If you have a bank balance, savings
   or and other capital, state total value £ ....

Expenses

6. Rent and Rates/Mortgage and Rates   £ .... per week/month

7. Hire purchase, bank loans   £ .... per week/month

8. Travelling expenses to and from work   £ .... per week/month

9. Other payments (give details)   £ .... per week/month

151

10. If you wish to say anything else about
your financial position, use this
space.

Signed . . . .
Address . . . .
This form was signed by the above-mentioned person before me at . . . . . .
. . . .
on the . . . . day of . . . . 19 . . . .
Signature . . . .
Full name . . . .
Description . . . .
*The followng persons may witness this form:
In England and Wales: a Justice of the Peace, Justices' Clerk or Solicitor
In Scotland: a Justice of the Peace, Sheriff or Solicitor
In Northern Ireland: a Justice of the Peace or Solicitor
Outside the U.K.: any person for the time being authorised by law
in the place where the document is executed to
administer an oath for any judicial or other legal
purpose;
a British consular officer;
a Notary Public;
if the person executing the document is serving
in any of the regular armed forces of the Crown,
an officer holding a commission in any of those
forces.

11. Complaint for order under Section 7 (DPMC Act 1978 ss. 7, 30(2)) (Rule 5(1))

. . . . MAGISTRATES' COURT (Code)
Date: . . . .
Respondent: . . . .
Address: . . . .
The Application of: . . . .
Address: . . . .
Telephone No. . . . .

who applies for an Order for financial provision under Section 7 of the
Domestic Proceedings and Magistrates' Courts Act 1978, not exceeding the
aggregate of the payments made to the Applicant during the last three
months; and states that [he] [she] has been living apart from [his] [her]
[husband] [wife] for a continuous period exceeding three months, neither of
them having deserted the other, and that [his] [her] [husband] [wife] has
been making periodical payments for [his] [her] benefit [and] [the benefit of

....
.... (name(s))
being a child/children of the family].

The aggregate amount of the payments made during the last three months
is £................

Taken before me

Justice of the Peace
Justices' Clerk

12. Notice to parent of child (other than a party to the marriage) of Court's power to make provision with regard to children (DPMC Act 1978, s.12) (Rule 9(2))

.... MAGISTRATES' COURT (Code)
Date: ....
To: ....
YOU ARE HEREBY GIVEN NOTICE that proceedings are pending under Part I
of the Domestic Proceedings and Magistrates' Courts Act 1978 between:
.... (the Applicant) and
.... (the Respondent)
and it has been stated that their family includes a child ....
(*name*) whose parents are .... (*name*) and
yourself but who has been treated as one of the family by the said Applicant
and Respondent.

If the information is correct, the Court has power to make provision at the
hearing for any of the following purposes as regards that child:

(a) legal custody (which may be awarded to either party or to a third
person, including yourself);

(b) access to the child by either or both of the parties or yourself, or any
other parent;

(c) on the application of a grandparent of the child, access to the child by
that grandparent;

(d) the payment of maintenance for the child by either or both of the
parties.

In certain exceptional circumstances the Court may commit the care of the
child to the Local Authority or place him under the supervision of the Local
Authority or a Probation Officer.

The hearing will take place on .... (*date*) at
.... (*time*) before the Magistrates' Court at ....
....

At the hearing the Court will hear anything which you may, as a parent of
the child, wish to say on these matters. For this purpose you may appear in
person or be represented by a barrister or solicitor.

Justices' Clerk

You should complete the tear-off slip below and return it as soon as possible.

The Clerk to the Justices,

.... Magistrates' Court

Address...

Proceedings between .... (*name*)

and .... (*name*)

Hearing date ....

I will/will not appear at the hearing or be represented.

I wish to speak to the court about custody and access.

Signed .... Date ....

13. Notice to parties to the marriage of Court's powers to make provision with regard to children (MC (MP) Rules 1980, r.8) (Rule 8)

Parties to proceedings under Part I of the Domestic Proceedings and Magistrates' Courts Act 1978 are informed that at the hearing the Court has power to make provision for any of the following purposes as regards any child of both parties or any child who has been treated by both parties as one of the family:

(a) legal custody (which may be awarded to either party or to a third person);

(b) access to the child by either or both of the parties (or anybody else who is a parent of the child);

(c) on the application of a grandparent of the child, access to the child by that grandparent;

(d) the payment of maintenance for the child by either or both of the parties.

In certain exceptional circumstances the court may commit the care of the child to a local authority or place him under the supervision of a local authority or a probation officer.

The Court may exercise these powers whether the applicant asks for any provision about the child or not and whether any other order is made on the application or the application is dismissed.

At the hearing of the application the Court will hear anything the parties may wish to say on these matters.

The Court cannot make its final decision on the application until it has decided whether or not, and if so how, to exercise these powers.

Justices' Clerk

.................................Magistrates' Court

Address...

14. Complaint for Family Protection Order

.... MAGISTRATES' COURT (Code)
Date: ....
Respondent:..
Address: ....
Substance of complaint: ....
....

And the applicant applies for an order under section 16 of the Domestic Proceedings and Magistrates' Courts Act 1978, namely that:

[The respondent shall not use, or threaten to use, violence against the person of the applicant [and that the respondent shall not incite or assist any other person to use, or threaten to use, violence against the person of the applicant].]

[The respondent shall not use, or threaten to use, violence against the person[s] of ....
of..
being [a child] [children] of the family [and that the respondent shall not incite or assist any other person to use, or threaten to use, violence against the person[s] of ....
of ....].]

[The respondent shall leave ....
being the matrimonial home [and that the respondent shall permit the applicant to enter and remain therein].]

[The respondent shall not enter ....
being the matrimonial home [and that the respondent shall permit the applicant to enter and remain therein].]

[The costs of the court and of the applicant shall be paid by the respondent.]

The complaint of .... (the applicant)
Address: ....
Telephone number: ....
who states that the particulars given above are true.

Taken before me,

Justice of the Peace
Justices' Clerk

15. Notice to Respondent of Court's powers with regard to Family Protection Orders (DPMC Act 1978, ss.16, 18(1)) (Rule 10)

Applications for an Order under Section 16

Respondents to an application for an Order under Section 16 of the Domestic Proceedings and Magistrates' Courts Act 1978 are informed that on hearing the application the Court (if satisfied as to certain circumstances involving violence or threats of violence) has power to make any Order under Section 16 of the Act, whether or not the Applicant asks for a particular kind of Order to be made and, if so, whether or not the particular kind of Order asked for by the applicant is made.

Any or all of the following Orders may be made under Section 16:—

(i) *Under Section 16(2)*
   (*a*) An order that the Respondent shall not use, or threaten to use, violence against the person of the applicant;
   (b) An Order that the Respondent shall not use, or threaten to use, violence against the person of a child of the family.

(ii) *Under Section 16(3)*
   (*a*) An Order requiring the Respondent to leave the matrimonial home;
   (*b*) An Order prohibiting the Respondent from entering the matrimonial home.

(iii) *Under Section 16(4)*
   If an Order under Section 16(3) is made, a further Order requiring the Respondent to permit the Applicant to enter and remain in the matrimonial home.

(iv) *Under Section 16(10)*
   If an Order under Section 16(2) is made, it may include provision that the Respondent shall not incite or assist another person to use, or threaten to use, violence against the person of the Applicant or, as the case may be, the child of the family.

Powers of arrest under Section 18

In certain circumstances the Court may attach a power of arrest to an Order made under Section 16. If so, a constable may arrest the Respondent without warrant if he has reasonable cause for suspecting the Respondent of being in breach of the Order.

16. Application for warrant of arrest for breach of family protection order

.... MAGISTRATES' COURT (Code)

Date: ....

Respondent:..

Address: ....

The .... Magistrates' Court on .... 19 ..... made an Order under Section 16 of the Domestic Proceedings and Magistrates' Courts Act 1978 [last varied on .... 19 .....] to which the court did not attach a power of arrest.

And the respondent has disobeyed the said order and is in breach of the same in that (*Insert particulars*)

And the applicant now applies for a Warrant for the arrest of the respondent to be issued under section 18(4) of the Domestic Proceedings and Magistrates' Courts Act 1978.

The application of ....

Address: ....

Telephone number: ....

Who upon [oath] [affirmation] states that the particulars given above are true.

Taken and [sworn] [affirmed] before me,

Justice of the Peace
Justices' Clerk

17. Complaint: Custody (Guardianship of Minors Act 1971)

.... MAGISTRATES' COURT (Code)

Complainant: ....

Address: ....

Defendant: ....

Address: ....

COMPLAINT: Application for Order for the custody [and maintenance] of the child[ren]:

.... born ....

[.......................... born ....]

[.......................... born ....]

[.......................... born ....]

of which the said .... is the [mother] [father] and the defendant is the [father] [mother]

Solicitors: for the complainant ....

....

for the defendant ....

....

(Signed) .... (Complainant)

Dated ....

Clerk of the Court

Date of hearing: ....

18. Complaint: Affiliation (before birth)

.... MAGISTRATES' COURT (Code)

The Complaint of: ....

single woman, residing at ....

who upon [oath] [affirmation] states that she is now with child and that

....

of ....

is the father of such child, and she applies for a summons to be served upon him to answer to the said complaint.

(Signed) .... (Complainant)

Taken and [sworn] [affirmed] before me, this......... day of........

Justice of the Peace

19. Complaint: affiliation (after birth)

.... MAGISTRATES' COURT (Code)

The complaint of ....

single woman, of...

who states that she was delivered of an illegitimate child on the.........

day of .... 19 ....., and alleges that ....

of..

is the father of such child, and having given proof on oath that he did within three years next after the birth of such child pay money for its maintenance, she applies for a summons to be served upon him to answer the said complaint.

[I acknowledge receipt of a notice re *Blood Tests*]

(Signed) .... (Complaintant)

Taken before me, this .... day of .... 19 .....

Justice of the Peace

20. Complaint for custodianship order

.... MAGISTRATES' CODE (Code)

Date .... 19 .....

Matter of Complaint:

An application for a custodianship order under section 33(1) of the Children Act 1975

Delete words in square brackets as necessary

[an application for maintenance payments if a custodianship order is made]

[an application for variation of a maintenance order made

Specify court

at...

on.......... 19 ..... in the amount of £...........

payable to......................................]

1. Particulars of complainant(s)

Name: ....

158

Enter the address where the complainant has his/her home and the place (if different) where documents may be received.

Address: ....
....
Date of birth: .... 19 .....
Occupation: ....
Relationship (if any) to the child in respect of whom the custodianship order is sought: .
[Name of joint complainant: ....
Address: ....
....
Date of birth: .... 19 .....
Occupation: ....
Relationship (if any) to the child in respect of whom the custodianship order is sought: ....]

2. Particulars of child
Name: ....
Sex: .... Date of birth .... 19 .....

If the child is illegitimate give details of the putative father. If he has legal custody of the child by virtue of a court order give details of that order under paragraph 10.

3. Parentage
The child is the child of (name).....................
[of (address) ....
....]
[deceased]
[and (name) ....]
[of (address) ....
....]
[deceased]

Cross out this paragraph if the child has no guardian. Do not include the person who has custody of the child only.

[4. Guardian
The guardian(s) of the child (other than the mother or father of the child)
[is] [are] (name) ....
of address ....
....
[and (name) ....
of (address)..
....].]

Cross out the paragraphs which do not apply.
No consent is required where:
(a) The child has lived with the applicant(s) for a period or periods which amount to three years including the three months before the application is made or
(b) The applicant is either a relative or step-parent with whom the child has lived for three months before the application is made, or a person with whom the child has lived for a period or periods which

5. Consent of person(s) having legal custody
[(name) ....
of (address)..
....
[and (name) ....
of (address)..
....]
consent(s) to the making of a custodianship order in [my] [our] favour]
OR
[No-one has legal custody of the child]
OR
[I, (name) ....
have legal custody of the child]

amount to one year including the three months before the application is made AND (in both cases) no person has legal custody of the child, the applicant has legal custody of the child or the person having legal custody of the child cannot be found.

OR
[the person who has legal custody of the child cannot be found]

Cross out this paragraph unless the child is in the care of a local authority or a voluntary organisation.

[6. Care
The child is in the care of ....
....
[who has/have the powers and duties of a parent or guardian of the child]
[who has/have parental rights and duties in respect of the child].]

If paragraph 6 is crossed out, this paragraph must be completed.

[7. Local Authority
The name and address of the local authority in whose area the child resides is ....
of ....,
....]

Cross out this paragraph unless some person or body has to pay maintenance for the child under a court order or agreement.

[8. Maintenance
[Under a court order made on .... 19 .....
at ....]
[by an agreement dated .... 19 .....]
(name) ....
of (address)....................................
....
is obliged to pay maintenance for the child.]

General particulars
9. The child has lived with [me] [us] [continuously since the .... day of ....19 .....]
[for the following periods.........................
....
....]
and has therefore lived with [me] [us] for ....
[months] [years] including the three months immediately before the making of this application.

10. No proceedings wholly or partially relating to the child have been commenced or completed in any court in England and Wales or elsewhere [except ....
....
....
....]

The complaint of the above-named complainant
Taken [and sworn] before me

Justice of the Peace
Justices' Clerk

ANNEX

You should complete the tear-off slip attached and submit it to the justices' clerk so that he may send it within seven days after the making of your complaint (or such extended period as the court or local authority may allow) to the local authority in whose area the child resides. The local authority is required to arrange for an officer of the authority to make a report to the court in connection with your application for a custodianship order; you should give the names and addresses of two referees whom the officer of the local authority may approach.

NOTICE OF AN APPLICATION FOR
A CUSTODIANSHIP ORDER

Date: .... 19 .....

To the .... Council

....

Notice is hereby given that a complaint has been made by [me] [us] on .... 19 .....

to a Justice of the Peace acting for

Petty sessions area

....

Name of child   for a custodianship order in relation to ....

....

Address   of ....

....

Name of complainant(s): ....

....

Address (if different from that above): ....

....

....

For the purpose of this application reference may be made to:—

Name of first referee: ....

Address: ....

....

Name of second referee: ....

Address: ....

....

21. Medical certificate for child or complainant in application for custodianship order

Tick the appropriate box

I examined ☐ the above-mentioned child
☐ the complainant

on the .... day of .... 19 .....

Tick the appropriate box

☐ I have formed the opinion that he/she is not suffering from any ill-health, disability or abnormality.

☐ he/she is suffering from

Where the person being examined is suffering from any ill-health, disability or abnormality give details of its nature and extent and its likely prognosis.

....
....
....

Signed.................. Date .... 19 .....
Name (in block capitals)............................
Qualifications......................................
Address ....
....

22. Application for an adoption order

The application must be made to a domestic court within whose area the child is.

To the .... DOMESTIC COURT.

Enter the first name(s) and surname of the child as shown in any certificate referred to in paragraph 6 below; otherwise enter the first name(s) and surname by which the child was known before being placed for adoption.

Delete words in square brackets as necessary

I/We, the undersigned,............................
[and...]
wishing to adopt...................................,
a child, hereby give the following further particulars in support of my/our application.

PART 1

Particulars of the applicant(s)

Insert the address where the applicant has his/her home and the place (if different) where documents may be served upon him/her.

1. Name and address, etc.
Name of [first] applicant in full ....
....
Address ....
....
Occupation ....
Date of Birth .... 19 .....
Relationship (if any) to the child...................
[Name of [second] applicant in full ....
....
Address ....
....
Occupation ....
Date of Birth .... 19 .....

Relationship (if any) to the child ....]

2. Domicile
[I am] [We are] [One of us namely ....
.... is] domiciled
in [England and Wales] [Scotland] [Northern Ireland] [the
Channel Islands] [the Isle of Man].

3. Status
[We are married to each other and our marriage certificate
(or other evidence of marriage) is attached] OR
[I am unmarried/a widow/a widower/a divorcee] OR
[I am applying alone as a married person and can satisfy
the court that

....
....
....
....
....]

Documentary evidence of marital status should be supplied. A married applicant can apply alone if he or she can satisfy the court that his or her spouse cannot be found, or that they have separated and are living apart and that the separation is likely to be permanent, or that by reason of physical or mental ill health the spouse is incapable of making an application for an adoption order. Any documentary evidence on which the applicant proposes to rely should be attached to the application. The name and address (if known) of the spouse should be supplied and the marriage certificate (or other evidence of marriage) should be attached.

[4. I am applying alone for an adoption order in respect of
my own child and can satisfy the court that the other
natural parent ....
....
....
....
....]

State the reason to be relied upon, e.g. that the other natural parent is dead, or cannot be found, or that there is some other reason, which should be specified, justifying his or her exclusion. Documentary evidence, e.g. a death certificate should be supplied where appropriate.

[5. Health
A report on my/our health, made by a registered medical
practitioner, on the......... day of......... 19 .....
is attached.]

A separate health report is required in respect of each applicant, and the report must have been made during the period of three months before the date of the application. No report is required, however, if the child was placed for adoption with the applicant by an adoption agency or if he/she is the child of the applicant or either of them.

163

PART 2

Particulars of the child

If the child has previously been adopted, a certified copy of the entry in the Adopted Children Register should be attached and not a certified copy of the original entry in the Registers of Births. Where a certificate is not attached enter the place, including the country, of birth if known.

6. Identity etc. The child is of the [male] [female] sex and is not and has not been married.
[He] [She] [was born on the.........................
day of .... 19 ..... and is the person to whom the attached [birth] [adoption] certificate relates.] OR
[was born on or about the.......... day of ....
19 ..... in.......................................]
[He] [She] is a .... national.

The report must have been made during the period of three months before the date of the application. No report is required, however, if the child was placed for adoption with the applicant by an adoption agency, or if he/she is the child of the applicant or either of them.

[7. Health.
A report on the health of the child, made by a registered medical practitioner, on the ....
day of .... 19 ....., is attached.]

The order made by the court freeing the child for adoption and any order made under section 23 should be attached.

[8. The child is free for adoption pursuant to section 14 of the Children Act 1975, and I/We attach hereto the order of the..
.... court,
dated .... 19 ....., to that effect.
The parental rights and duties relating to the child were thereby vested in
....
[and were transferred to ....
by order of the .... Court
under section 23 of the Children Act 1975
on .... 19 ....].]

This paragraph and paragraphs 10 to 14 only apply if the child is not free for adoption. If the child has previously been adopted, give the names of his/her adoptive parents and not those of his/her natural parents. If the child is illegitimate and the putative father has legal custody of the child by virtue of a court order, give details of that order under paragraph 19.

[9. Parentage etc. The child is the child of
....]
[whose last known address was ....
....]
[deceased]
and...
[whose last known address was ....
....]
[deceased].]

Delete this paragraph if the child has no guardian. Enter particulars of any person appointed by deed or will in accordance with the provisions of the Guardianship of Infants Acts 1886 and

[10. The guardian(s) of the child (other than the mother or father of the child) [is] [are]
....
of ....
....
[and ....

1925 or the
Guardianship of
Minors Act 1971, or
by a court of
competent jurisdiction
to be a guardian. Do
not include any person
who has the custody
of the child only.

of ....
....].]

Enter either in
paragraph 11 or 12 the
names of the persons
mentioned in
paragraphs 9 and 10,
except that in the case
of an illegitimate child
the name of the father
of the child should be
entered only if he has
custody of the child by
virtue of a court
order.
Where it is sought to
dispense with parental
agreement, enter in
paragraph 12 one or
more of the grounds
set out in section 12(2)
of the 1975 Act.

[11. Parental agreement. I/We understand that the said
....
[and ....]
[is] [are] willing to agree to the making of an adoption
order in pursuance of my/our application.]

[12. I/We request the court to dispense with the agreement
of
....
[and ....]
on the grounds that ....
....
....
[and ....
....]
and there are attached hereto three copies of a statement
of the facts on which I/We intend to rely.]

This paragraph should
be completed where
the child is in the care
of a local authority or
a voluntary
organisation.

[13. Care etc. The child is in the care of ....
....
who have the [powers and duties of a parent or guardian
of the child] [the parental rights and duties in respect of
the child].]

This paragraph should
be completed where
some person or body
is liable to contribute
to the maintenance of
the child under a court
order or agreement.

[14. Maintenance. ....
of ....
....
is liable [by virtue of an order made by the ....
court at ....
on the .... day of .... 19 .....]
[by an agreement dated the ....
day of .... 19 .....] to contribute
to the maintenance of the child.]

15. Proposed names. If an adoption order is made in
pursuance of this application, the child is to be known by
the following names:
Surname ....
Other names ....

PART 3

Under section 9 of the
1975 Act, an adoption
order cannot be made
unless the child has
had his/her home with
the applicants or one
of them:— (a) for at
least 13 weeks if the
applicant or one of

General
16. The child has lived with me/us continuously since
the .... day of .... 19 .....
[and has accordingly had his/her home with me/us for the
five years preceding the date of this application].

165

them is a parent, step-parent or relative of the child or if the child was placed with the applicant by an adoption agency or in pursuance of an order of the High Court; (b) for at least 12 months in any other case.

17. The child was [placed with me/us for adoption on the................ day of................ 19 .....
by ....,
an adoption agency] OR [received into my/our actual custody in the following circumstances:

....
....
....
....]

Notice does not have to be given if the child was placed with the applicant by an adoption agency. Where notice does have to be given, no order can be made until the expiration of 3 months from the date of the notice.

The nature of the proceedings and the date and effect of any orders made should be stated. The court cannot proceed with the application if a previous application made by the same applicant in relation to the child was refused, unless one of the conditions in section 22(4) of the 1975 Act is satisfied. The court must dismiss the application if it considers that, where the application is made by a married couple of whom one is a parent and the other a step-parent of the child, or by a step-parent of the child alone, the matter would be better dealt with under section 42 (orders for custody etc. in matrimonial proceedings) of the Matrimonial Causes Act 1973.

[18. I/We/One of us namely ....
notified the ....
Council on the.............. day of..............
19 ..... of my/our intention to apply for an adoption order in respect of the child.]

19. No proceedings relating in whole or in part to the child other than as stated in paragraph 8 have been completed or commenced in any court in England and Wales or else-where [except ....
....
....
....
....
....]

20. I/We have not received or given any payment or reward for, or in consideration of, the adoption of the child, for any agreement to the making of an adoption order, the transfer of the actual custody of the child with a view to adoption or the making of any arrangements for adoption [except as follows:— ....
....
....
....]

Enter the name and address of the adoption agency or individual who took part in the arrangements for placing the child for adoption in the actual custody of the applicant.

21. As far as I/we know, the only person(s) or body(ies) who have taken part in the arrangements for the child's adoption are ....

....

....

....

Where the applicant or one of the applicants is a parent of the child, or a relative as defined by section 57 (1) of the Adoption Act 1958 (as amended) or the child was placed with the applicant by an adoption agency, no referee need be named.

[22. For the purpose of this application reference may be made to

....

of ....

....]

If the applicant wishes his/her identity to be kept confidential, the serial number obtained under rule 14 should be given.

[23. I/We desire that my/our identity should be kept confidential, and the serial number of this application is ....]

I/We accordingly apply for an adoption order in respect of the child.

Dated this............. day of............. 19 .....

Signature(s)............................

....

23. Notice of appeal against conviction/sentence to Crown Court

To:
The Justices' Clerk,
The Magistrates' Court,

....

And to:...

of .... (the prosecutor)

I, ...

of...

do hereby give you and each of you notice that it is my intention at the .... Crown Court, to appeal against [my sentence on] a certain conviction of me by the .... Magistrates' Court on the .... day of.... 19 ..... for having on the.... day of.... 19 .....

AND that the general grounds of such appeal are

and that I am not guilty of the said offence [that my sentence of . . . .
. . . . was too severe].
Dated this . . . . day of . . . . 19 . . . . .
   (Signed) . . . .

Notice must be served on the Justices' Clerk and on the prosecutor within 21 days of conviction or sentence.

Appendix 2

Practice Directions, Practice Notes and Guidelines

1. Practice Note: Submission of no case
[1962] 1 All ER 448

Those of us who sit in the Divisional Court have the distinct impression that justices today are being persuaded all too often to uphold a submission of no case. In the result, this court has had on many occasions to send the case back to the justices for the hearing to be continued with inevitable delay and increased expenditure. Without attempting to lay down any principle of law, we think that as a matter of practice justices should be guided by the following considerations.

A submission that there is no case to answer may properly be made and upheld:

   (a) when there has been no evidence to prove an essential element in the alleged offence;
   (b) when the evidence adduced by the prosecution has been so discredited as a result of cross-examination or is so manifestly unreliable that no reasonable tribunal could safely convict on it.

Apart from these two situations a tribunal should not in general be called on to reach a decision as to conviction or acquittal until the whole of the evidence which either side wishes to tender has been placed before it. If, however, a submission is made that there is no case to answer, the decision should depend not so much on whether the adjudicating tribunal (if compelled to do so) would at that stage convict or acquit but on whether the evidence is such that a reasonable tribunal might convict. If a reasonable tribunal might convict on the evidence so far laid before it, there is a case to answer.

Parker CJ

2. Identification evidence: Attorney-General's Guidelines
[Written answer of the Attorney-General to the House of Commons 27 May 1976]

" . . . The Director (of Public Prosecutions) and I have reviewed the whole area of identification evidence and procedure in order to establish whether, without prejudice to decisions as to changes in the law or practice, we can introduce in the handling of such cases, before and at the trial, still further safeguards against the danger of wrong conviction due to misidentification. We have now agreed upon the following guidelines in cases in which it appears likely that identification will be an issue.

1. All cases of which the Director has the conduct will be given the personal consideration of the Director himself or his Deputy and will, if the Director considers it desirable, be reported to the Law Officers. Such cases will be kept under review in the light of any new developments.

2. The procedure under section 1 of the Criminal Justice Act 1967 (Committal, with the consent of the defence, by magistrates without consideration of the evidence) will not be used. Instead, the witness as to identity will be called to give oral evidence, and it will, of course, be open to the accused himself, at the committal stage, to challenge that evidence and to give evidence of any alibi, and call witnesses to support it. Should, however, there have been no prior opportunity for the police to inquire into such an alibi, it might then be necessary for the Director to seek an adjournment of the committal proceedings for an investigation to be made. If the alibi were substantiated the proceedings could be brought to an end.

3. The Director's representative at the committal proceedings, or Crown counsel at any subsequent trial, will not invite a witness as to identity, who has not previously identified the accused at an identification parade, to make a dock identification unless the witness's attendance at a parade was unnecessary or impracticable, or there are exceptional circumstances.

4. Any failure to comply with the current Home Office guidance, or any which may replace it, as to the manner of holding identification parades, or of showing to potential witnesses photographs of a suspect, will continue to be regarded as an important factor in considering whether or not to institute or, as the case may be, continue proceedings.

5. Where proceedings are instituted, the Director will, subject to the requirements of the public interest, continue his practice of making available to the defence any material likely to assist the

defence. In particular he will supply to the accused's solicitors on request the name and address of any witness, whether or not such witness has attended an identification parade, who is known to him as having stated that he saw, or as being likely to have seen, the criminal in the circumstances of the crime, together with a copy of any description of the criminal given by such a person.

In cases not referred to the Director neither he nor I can ensure that these safeguards will be adopted. I very much hope, however, that, pending legislation or judicial guidance, they will be generally accepted and that the Director's advice will be sought in difficult or borderline cases. The Director and I are confident that magistrates and their clerks will fully co-operate in implementing the practice of calling oral evidence of identification at the committal stage."

Note also the following further written answer of the Attorney-General to the House of Commons 25 July 1979:

"While I am satisfied that, in cases referred to the Director of Public Prosecutions, the guidelines have been generally effective in the safeguarding against the danger of wrong conviction due to misidentification, experience has shown that rigid adherence to the requirement for witnesses as to identity being called to give oral evidence at the lower court is unnecessary and can itself lead to injustice. For example, in one case of alleged murder, where the defence would have been content with the procedure under section 1 of the Criminal Justice Act 1967 — committal by magistrates without consideration of the evidence — the court in question was unable to find time for a full hearing until a date when the trial itself might otherwise have been expected. In other instances, child victims of sexual assaults have had to undergo the ordeal again unwished for by the defence, of giving evidence at both committal proceedings and the subsequent trial. After careful consideration, therefore, I have decided that the guidelines should be modified so that, where neither the prosecution nor the defence feel it necessary for witnesses as to identity to give oral evidence at committal proceedings, and provided the court agrees, the procedure under section 1 of the 1967 Act may be used. I have also found that the Director and his deputy are obliged to give unnecessary personal consideration to straightforward cases and again I propose to modify the guidelines to provide that all cases of which the Director has the conduct will be considered at not less level than principal assistant director. I would repeat the hope of my predecessor, that other prosecutors will accept these guidelines and that the Director's advice will be sought in difficult or borderline cases."

3. Practice Direction: functions of justices' clerk
[1981] 1 All ER 831, [1981] 1 WLR 1163

1. A justices' clerk is responsible to the justices for the performance of any of the functions set out below by any member of his staff acting as court clerk and may be called in to advise the justices even when he is not personally sitting with the justices as clerk to the court.

2. It shall be the responsibility of the justices' clerk to advise the justices as follows: (a) on questions of law or of mixed law and fact; (b) as to matters of practice and procedure.

3. If it appears to him necessary to do so, or he is so requested by the justices, the justices' clerk has the responsibility to (a) refresh the justices' memory as to any matter of evidence and to draw attention to any issues involved in the matters before the court, (b) advise the justices generally on the range of penalties which the law allows them to impose and on any guidance relevant to the choice of penalty provided by the law, the decisions of the superior courts or other authorities. If no request for advice has been made by the justices, the justices' clerk shall discharge his responsibility in court in the presence of the parties.

4. The way in which the justices' clerk should perform his functions should be stated as follows. (a) The justices are entitled to the advice of their clerk when they retire in order that the clerk may fulfil his responsibility outlined above. (b) Some justices may prefer to take their own notes of evidence. There is, however, no obligation on them to do so. Whether they do so or not, there is nothing to prevent them from enlisting the aid of their clerk and his notes if they are in any doubt as to the evidence which has been given. (c) If the justices wish to consult their clerk solely about the evidence or his notes of it, this should ordinarily, and certainly in simple cases, be done in open court. The object is to avoid any suspicion that the clerk has been involved in deciding issues of fact.

5. For the reasons stated in the Practice Direction of 15th January 1954 ([1954] 1 All ER 230, [1954] 1 WLR 213), which remains in full force and effect, in domestic proceedings it is more likely than not that the justices will wish to consult their clerk. In particular, where rules of court require the reasons for their decision to be drawn up in consultation with the clerk, they will need to receive his advice for this purpose.

6. This Practice Direction is issued with the concurrence of the President of the Family Division.

2 July 1981   Lane CJ

[Note: A court clerk is entitled to give advice on a point of law to justices who had not requested advice. It was wrong for a clerk to sit mute and immobile in court if he thought the justices were proceedings on an erroneous basis of law. Para. 3 above was not referable to the clerk's obligation to advise, but to refreshing the justices' memory: *R* v *Uxbridge Justices exp. Smith* (1985).]

4. Practice Direction: presence of justices' clerk in retiring room (matrimonial cases)
[1954] 1 All ER 230, [1954] 1 WLR 213

In a statement made in the Divisional Court of the Queen's Bench Division on 16 November 1953 ([1953] 2 All E.R. 1306) about clerks to justices being present when the justices have retired to consider their decision, Lord Goddard CJ said (ibid 1307) that the ruling of that court did not apply to justices when exercising jurisdiction in matrimonial cases as they were then subject to the directions and control of this Division. Before making any pronouncement in response to several requests for a ruling by this court on the subject, I wished to consult the judges of this Division. I now have their authority to say that they agree with the statement I am about to make. I am also authorised by Lord Simonds LC to say that he approves of it. Vaisey J also asks me to say that he agrees with it.

I wish to say at the outset that it rarely happens that an allegation of undue interference by the clerk in the decision of a complaint under the Summary Jurisdiction (Separation and Maintenance) Acts, 1895 to 1949, is made a ground of appeal to this Divisional Court. Nevertheless, it is at least as important in cases of this class as in cases of other classes dealt with by courts of summary jurisdiction that the decision should be that of the justices themselves and not that of the justices and their clerk, and that, not only should this be so in fact, but that nothing should be done to give the parties or the public the impression that the clerk is influencing the decision. I am, therefore, in complete agreement with Lord Goddard CJ that it should not be regarded as a matter of course that, if justices retire to consider their decision, the clerk should retire with them. Moreover, whether the justices invite the clerk to retire with them or send for him in the course of their deliberations, I agree that the clerk should always return to his place in court as soon as the justices release him, leaving them to complete their deliberations alone. Bearing in mind that domestic proceedings are often lengthy and may involve points of law in relation to the complaint itself or to the amount of maintenance, and that this court insists that a proper note of the evidence must be kept, and that, in the event of an appeal, justices must be prepared to state the reasons for their decision, I recognise that more often than not justices may properly wish to refresh their recollection of the evidence by recourse to the clerk's note, or to seek his advice about the law, before coming to their decision.

Having regard to the high standard of care which is generally shown by courts of summary jurisdiction in dealing with these domestic proceedings, I do not think it is necessary for me to say more than that I am confident that justices taking part in them may be trusted to act, and to ensure that they appear to act, on the fundamental principle that they alone are the judges.

15 January 1954   Merriman P

5. Practice Note: costs — acquitted accused
[1982] 3 All ER 1152, [1982] 1 WLR 1447

Under s.1 of the Costs in Criminal Cases Act 1973 a magistrates' court dealing summarily with an indictable offence and dismissing the information, or inquiring into any offence as examining justices and determining not to commit the accused for trial, may order the payment out of central funds of the costs of the defence. A similar power exists under s.12(1) of the 1973 Act where an information is not proceeded with.

Whether to make such an award is a matter in the unfettered discretion of the court in the light of the circumstances of each particular case.

It should be accepted as normal practice that such an award be made unless there are positive reasons for making a different order. Examples of such reasons are: (a) where the prosecution has acted spitefully or has instituted or continued proceedings without reasonable cause, the defendant's costs should be paid by the prosecutor under s.2 of the 1973 Act; if there is any doubt whether payment will be forthcoming from the prosecutor the position of the defendant should be protected by making an order for costs from central funds in his favour as well; (b) where the defendant's own conduct has brought suspicion on himself and has misled the prosecution into thinking that the case against him is stronger than it is, the defendant can be left to pay his own costs; (c) where there is ample evidence to support a conviction but the defendant is acquitted on a technicality which has no merit, again the defendant can be left to pay his own costs; (c) where there is ample evidence to support a conviction but the defendant is acquitted on a technicality which has no merit, again the defendant can be left to pay his own costs; (d) where the defendant is acquitted on one charge but convicted on another, the court should make whatever order seems just having regard to the relative importance of the two charges and the conduct of the parties generally.

25 November 1982   Lane CJ

6. Practice Direction: costs — disallowance
[1977] 1 All ER 540, [1977] 1 WLR 181

1.   Section 3(1) of the Costs in Criminal Cases Act 1973 provides that where a person is prosecuted or tried on indictment before the Crown Court the court may: (a) order the payment out of central funds of the costs of the prosecution; (b) if the accused is acquitted, order the payment out of central funds of the costs of the defence. Similar provision is made in s.3(2) in respect of appeals to the Crown Court against conviction or sentence, and s.18 extends s.3 to include other proceedings in the Crown Court. There is in addition a power to pay witnesses' expenses and to order that where the costs are awarded to the accused the costs incurred before examining justices may be included.

2.   The costs to be paid belong to the prosecutor or the accused, as the case my be, and are (s.3(3)):
     "such sums as appear to the Crown Court reasonably sufficient: To compensate the prosecutor, or as the case may be, the accused, for the expenses properly incurred by him in carrying on the proceedings".

3.   The amount of costs ordered to be paid are to be ascertained on taxation by the appropriate officer of the Crown Court (s.3(6)).

4.   In deciding whether to make an order for costs out of central funds the court should in the first instance have regard: (a) in the case of the prosecutor, to the principle that an order should normally be made unless the proceedings have been instituted or presented without reasonable cause; (b) in the case of an accused who has been acquitted, to the principle that in the exercise of its discretion the court will normally award costs out of central funds when it has power to do so in favour of a successful defendant unless there are positive reasons for making a different order. Examples of such

reasons are set out in the Practice Direction of 5 June 1973 [1973] 2 All ER 592, [1973] 1 WLR 718.

5. If after considering the matter on the principles set out in para 4 the court decides to make an order it nevertheless (a) must direct the appropriate officer to disallow the costs incurred in respect of any items if it is plain that those costs were not properly incurred; such costs are not payable under the 1973 Act, (b) may direct the appropriate officer to consider or investigate on taxation any items if it appears that the costs in respect of them may have been improperly incurred. Costs not properly incurred include costs in respect of work unreasonably done, eg if the case has been conducted unreasonably so as to incur unjustifiable expense, or costs have been wasted by failure to conduct the proceedings with reasonable competence and expedition. The precise terms of the order for costs and of any direction should be entered in the court record.

6. Where the court has in mind that a direction in accordance with para 5(a) or 5(b) might be given it should inform any party whose costs might be affected or his legal representative of the precise terms thereof and give a reasonable opportunity to show cause why no direction should be given. This should normally be done in chambers at such time as the court thinks proper. If the court decides to give a direction it may announce the decision in open court if of the opinion that it is in the interests of justice to do so. If a direction is given under para 5(b) the court should inform the party concerned of his right to make representations to the appropriate officer.

7. Whether or not any direction under para 5(a) or 5(b) has been given, the appropriate officer may consult the court on any matter touching the allowance or disallowance of costs. At this stage a direction under para 5(a) will not be appropriate.

8. If the court gives a direction under para 5(b) or a similar direction on being consulted under para 7, the appropriate officer should afford to any party whose costs may be adversely affected or his legal representative an opportunity to make representations in relation thereto.

9. On taxation the appropriate officer should have regard to: the terms of the order made and any direction given by the court; any representations in relation to them; all relevant information available to him from the court record, the documents in the case, or otherwise.

10. This Practice Direction does not apply to the payment of costs under the Legal Aid in Criminal Proceedings (Fees and Expenses) Regulations 1968, to orders for costs inter partes made under the Costs in Criminal Cases Act 1973, to costs awarded in civil proceedings by virtue of RSC O.62, nor to the exercise of the court's inherent jurisdiction to order a solicitor personally to pay the costs thrown away by his negligence (see *R v Smith Martin*) [1975] QB 531, [1974] 1 All ER 651).

7 February 1977   Widgery CJ

7. Practice Direction: matrimonial appeals — one judge — provinces
[1981] 1 All ER 400, [1981] 1 WLR 38

With effect from 12 January 1981, RSC O.56, rr.4A and 5 are amended so that appeals by case stated in any of the types of proceedings therein set out are taken by a single judge as a general rule and only by a Divisional Court of the Family Division if the court so directs (see RSC (Amendment No 4) 1980, SI 1980 No 2000, r.9(2)).

The rules require that all relevant papers be lodged in the Principal Registry of the Family Division, but there is no requirement in the rules that the single judge must be a single judge sitting in London. Accordingly, any party wishing the appeal to be heard and determined by a single judge outside London should apply to the President for a direction to this effect. The application should be made by letter addressed to the Clerk of the Rules. Where such a direction is given, the Clerk of the Rules will inform the appellant of the relevant divorce town and will refer the papers to the listing officer of the appropriate circuit office for a date of hearing to be fixed and notified to the appellant.

22 January 1981   R L Bayne-Powell, Senior Registrar

8. Practice Direction: Crime: evidence by written statements
(The Times 4 June 1986)

2. Where the prosecution proposes to tender written statements in evidence under either s.102 of the Magistrates' Courts Act 1980 or s.9 of the Criminal Justice Act 1968 it will frequently be not only proper but also necessary for the orderly presentation of the evidence for certain statements to be edited.

This will occur either because a witness has made more than one statement whose contents should conveniently be reduced into a single, comprehensive statement or where a statement contains inadmissible, prejudicial or irrelevant material.

Editing of statements should in all circumstances be done by a Crown Prosecutor (or by a legal representative, if any, of the prosecutor if the case is not being conducted by the Crown Prosecution Service) and not by a police officer.

3. Composite statements. A composite statement giving the combined effect of two or more earlier statements or settled by a person referred to in paragraph 2 above must be prepared in compliance with the requirements of s.102 of the 1980 Act or s.9 of the 1967 Act as appropriate and must then be signed by the witness.

4. Editing single statements. There are two acceptable methods of editing single statements:

(i) By marking copies of the statement in a way which indicates that the prosecution will not seek to adduce the evidence so marked. The original signed statement to be tendered to the court is not marked in any way.

The marking on the copy statement is done by lightly striking out the passages to be edited so that what appears beneath can still be read, or by bracketing, or by a combination of both. It is not permissible to produce a photocopy with the deleted material obliterated since this would be contrary to the requirement that the defence and the court should be served with copies of the signed original statement.

Whenever the striking out/bracketing method is used, it will assist if the following words appear at the foot or the frontispiece or index to any bundle of copy statements to be tendered: "The prosecution does not propose to adduce evidence of those passages of the attached copy statements which have been struck out and/or bracketed (Nor will it seek to do so at the trial unless a Notice of Further Evidence is served)".

(ii) By obtaining a fresh statement, signed by the witness, which omits the offending material, applying the above procedure in paragraph 3 above.

5. In most cases where a single statement is to be edited, the striking out/bracketing method will be the more appropriate, but the taking of a fresh statement is preferable in the following circumstances:

(a) When a police (or other investigating) officer's statement contains details of interviews with more suspects than are eventually charged, a fresh statement should be prepred and signed omitting all details of interview with those not charged except, in so far as it is relevant, for the bald fact that a certain named person was interviewed at a particular time, date and place.

(b) When a suspect is interviewed about more offences than are eventually made the subject of committal charges, a fresh statement should be prepared and signed omitting all questions and answers about the uncharged offences unless either they might appropriately be taken into consideration or evidence about those offences is admissible upon the charges preferred, such as evidence of system.

It may, however, be desirable to replace the omitted questions and answer with a phrase such as "After referring to some other matters, I then said . . . . " so as to make it clear that part of the interview has been omitted.

(c) A fresh statement should normally be prepared and signed if the only part of the original on which the prosecution are relying is only a small proportion of the whole although it remains desirable to use the alternative method if there is reason to believe that the defence might themselves wish to rely, in mitigation or for any other purpose, on at least some of those parts which the prosecution do not propose to adduce.

(d) When the passages contain material which the prosecution is entitled to withhold from disclosure to the defence.

6. Prosecutors should also be aware that, where statements are to be tendered under s.9 of the 1967 Act in the course of summary proceedings, there will be a greater need to prepare fresh statements excluding inadmissible or prejudicial material rather than using the striking out or bracketing method.

7. None of the above principles applies, in respect of committal proceedings, to documents which are exhibited (including statements under caution and signed contemporaneous notes). Nor do they apply to oral statements of a defendant which are recorded in the witness statements of interviewing police officers, except in the circumstances referred to in paragraph 5(b) above.

All this material should remain in its original state in the committal bundles, any editing being left to prosecuting counsel at the crown court (after discussion with defence counsel and, if appropriate, the trial judge).

8. Wherever a fresh statement is taken from a witness, a copy of the earlier, unedited statement(s) of that witness will be given to the defence in accordance with the Attorney General's Guidelines (Practice Note: Unused Material) [1982] 1 All ER 734) on the disclosure of the used material unless there are grounds under paragraph 6 of the guidelines for withholding such disclosure.

3 June 1986   Lane LCJ

Appendix 3

Tables

Table 1: Mode of trial procedure: changing the election

Change	Permissible?	Comments	
1. *From committal proceedings to summary trial*	At any time (MCA 1980 s.25(3)) but accused must consent	Court must have regard to representations by prosecutor (in accused's presence) or representations by accused. The nature of the case could make it more suitable for summary trial after all.	But if prosecution is by DPP, AG or SG his consent must be obtained.
2. *From summary trial to committal proceedings:*			
(a) Once unequivocal guilty plea has been accepted	Cannot be changed (*R* v *Dudley Magistrates' Court exp. Gillard* (1984)) No power to commit once a conviction is registered (*R* v *Grant* (1936))		
(b) Not guilty plea, no plea, or plea changed from guilty to not guilty	At any time before the close of the prosecution evidence (MCA 1980 s.25(2))	But the court has a discretion whether to allow the change (*R* v *Southampton JJ exp. Robins* (1980)). *Discretion to allow after change of plea: R* v *Southampton City JJ exp. Briggs* (1972): exercise of discretion depends on how the justices see the broad justice of the whole situation. *No automatic right*: may properly refuse to agree where, eg, court has	

Change	Permissible?	Comments
		already dealt with co-accused. Effect of the request upon other persons waiting to be tried is a valid consideration (*R* v *West Bromwich JJ exp. Pearson* (1981)).
		The court must pay attention to the accused's state of mind when he made the election. If the accused did not understand the nature and significance of the choice, it was as if he never made that choice. An important factor was whether or not he believed he had a defence. It looks as though an election for summary trial by an unrepresented accused would always be suspect in the Divisional Court, if legal representation later wanted a change to jury trial.
		The accused is not lightly to be deprived of a right to trial by jury regardless of whether the justices regard summary trial as more appropriate, even when he clearly elected summary trial once (*R* v *Birmingham JJ exp. Hodgson & Wiseman* (1985)).
		It must be clear that the accused understood the nature of the election. The Divisional Court held that an unrepresented 17-year old, no previous convictions, who said he did not understand the choice when he elected summary trial, should be allowed to re-elect jury trial (*R* v *Highbury Corner Magistrates' Court exp. Weekes* (1985)).
		Unless there is an abuse of the process the accused is entitled to have his application considered on its merits by the justices (*R* v *Warrington JJ exp. McDonagh* (1981)).
		When the court wishes to change from summary trial to indictment, it must not act precipitately and the change can only be effective once the summary trial has commenced: *R* v *Southend Justices exp. Wood* (1986).

Table 2: Changing the plea

Plea	Can plea be changed?		When?	Comments
Guilty	(a) Equivocal	Does not apply	Cannot accept a guilty plea	Plea to be treated as Not Guilty
	(b) Unequivocal— After sentence	No	Cannot be entertained after sentence	*R* v *Campbell exp. Hoy* (1953)
	(c) Unequivocal— Before sentence	Yes	Any time before sentence	The court has a discretion. It is for the court to decide if justice requires that the change should be permitted. It should only be exercised in clear cases and very sparingly (*S (an Infant) v Manchester City Recorder & Others* (1969)).
				It should only be allowed where justified by the interests of justice and not expediency (*R* v *Uxbridge JJ exp. Smith* (1977)).
				The accused pleaded guilty unequivocally to burglary and was remanded for legal representation. The court then refused an application to change plea and were upheld on appeal (*R* v *South Tameside Magistrates' Court exp. Rowland* (1984)).
Not guilty		Yes	At any time	The charge should be put to the defendant again and guilty plea taken (by accused preferably, and not his solicitor)

Table 3: Custodial sentence possibilities: Magistrates' Court

Sentence or order	Sentence Male	Female	Min. period	Max. period	Can it be suspended or partially suspended?	Comments
Prison	21 or over	21 or over	5 days	(Note 1) 6 months for indictable offence; 12 months if 2 or more indictable offences	Yes	Suspended sentence activated may be extra on normal maximum
Youth Custody	15-20	15-20	4 months & 1 day (Note 2)	As above (Note 2)	No	Absolute maximum is 12 months for under 17
Detention centre	14-20	No	21 days (Note 3)	4 months (at a time)	No	NOT after Youth Custody sentence unless special circumstances
Care of local authority	0-17	0-17	As decided by local authority or court on discharge application	Till 18	No	
Crown Court for sentence	17 upwards	17 upwards	—	As if convicted on indictment	—	

Notes:

(1) If the contravened statute provides a lesser maximum for an adult, that is the maximum.

(2) Youth custody is possible for less than 4 months and 1 day, but not less than 21 days when (a) the offender is a girl over 16, but not if 15 or 16 years old; (b) a boy has been to prison, borstal or youth custody before; (c) detention unsuitable because of the offender's mental or physical condition.

(3) Less than 21 days possible if guilty of breach of detention centre licence conditions.

(4) Under 21 — can be sentenced to be *detained* for fine default or contempt of court or kindred offence.

Table 4: Endorsable offences and maximum penalties

1.	Causing death by reckless driving s.1 RTA 1972	DD 70	Yes		Fine and/or 5 years	Indictable only
2.	Reckless driving s.2 RTA 1972	DD 30	No	10	Fine and/or 2 years £2000 and/or 6 months	Triable either way. Compulsory disqualification if committed within 3 years of previous conviction of offence 1 or 2 in this Table
3.	Careless driving or inconsiderate driving s.3 RTA 1972	CD 10 CD 20	No No	2—5 2—5	£1000 £1000	
4.	Driving, or attempting to when unfit through drink or drugs. s.5(1) RTA 1972	DR 20	Yes	10	£2000 and/or 6 months	3rd conviction (or 6 or 9a) in 10 years has 3 years minimum disqualification
5.	In charge when unfit through drink or drugs s.5(2) RTA 1972	DR 50	No		£1000 and/ or 3 months	
6.	Driving, or attempting to when blood alcohol exceeds the prescribed limit s.6(1)(A) RTA 1972	DR 10	Yes		£2000 and/ 6 months	Minister has prescribed limits: 80/100 — blood 107/100 — urine 35/100 — breath

185

Offence, Section and Act	D o E computer offence code	Compulsory disqualification (minimum 12 months except for special reasons)	Endorsement points	Maximum fine and/or imprisonment (offence committed on or after 1 May 1984) Magistrates' Court	Indictment	Remarks
7. In charge when alcohol level exceeds the prescribed limit s.6(1)(B) RTA 1972	DR 40	No	10	£1000 and/ or 3 months		
8. Failing to provide a specimen for a breath test s.7(4) RTA 1972	DR 70	No	4	£400		
9. Failing to provide a specimen for analysis, a. If driving or attempting to.	DR 30	Yes		£2000 and/ or 6 months		
b. In any other case s.8(7) RTA 1972	DR 60	No	10	£1000 and/ or 3 months		
10. Racing on a highway s.14 RTA 1972	MS 50	Yes		£1000		
11. Three on solo motor-cycle or pillion passenger in an unlawful position. s.16 RTA 1972	MS 20	No	1	£400		

12.	Failing to comply with traffic directions				
	a. Traffic light signals	TS10	No	3	£400	Prescribed by Regs. 31, 32, 33, Traffic Signs Regulations 1964
	b. Double white lines or continuous white line on nearside of dotted line, certain hatching.	TS 20	No	3	£400	Diagram 1013 It is suggested causing vehicle to stop on road where any of these markings has been placed is endorsable
	c. Stop sign	TS 30	No	3	£400	Diagram 601
	d. Directions of a constable or traffic warden	TS 40	No	3	£400	
	e. Drivers of large or slow vehicles 'phone for permission to cross s.22 RTA 1972	TS 50	No	3	£400	Diagram 649 *(Diagrams are in the Traffic Signs Regulations and General Directions 1975)*
13.	Parking in a dangerous position s.24 RTA 1972	MS 10	No	3	£400	
14.	Accident:					Where convictions for both offences arise from the same accident they are 'on the same occasion' for points purposes (*Johnson* v *Finbow*, The Times, March 21 1983)
	a. Failing to stop after	AC 10	No	5—9	£2000	
	b. Failing to report s.25 RTA 1972	AC 20	No	4—9	£2000	

Offence, Section and Act	D o E computer offence code	Compulsory disqualification (minimum 12 months except for special reasons)	Endorsement points	Maximum fine and/or imprisonment (offence committed on or after 1 May 1984) Magistrates' Court	Indictment	Remarks
15. Using or causing or permitting use of a motor vehicle or trailer:						
a. with defective brakes	CU 10	No	3	£1000, but £2000 in case of goods vehicle		If offender proves he had no knowledge and no reasonable cause to suspect that offence committed the court should not endorse or disqualify (Sch. 4 RTA 1972)
b. causing or likely to cause danger by reason of its condition, or the condition of its parts or accessories (excluding brakes, steering or tyres)	CU 20	No	3	£1000 but £2000 in case of goods vehicle		Every defect in every type constitutes a separate offence (*Saines v Woodhouse* [1970] All ER 388)
c. with defective tyres	CU 30	No	3	£1000 but £2000 in case of goods vehicle		
d. with defective steering	CU 40	No	3	£1000 but £2000 in case of goods vehicle		

Offence	Code	Disqualification	Penalty points	Fine	Notes
e. causing or likely to cause danger by reason of load or passengers s.40(6) RTA 1972	CU 50	No	3	£1000 but £2000 in case of goods vehicle	
16. Driving with no licence, where no licence could be granted or if only provisional licence could be granted and conditions on it would not have been complied with s.84 RTA 1972	LC 10	No	2	£400	Failure to renew full, non provisional licence does not attract disqualification/ endorsement. Causing or permitting a person to commit this offence is a separate offence, and is not endorsable (S.84(2) RTA 1972)
17. Failing to comply with conditions of a provisional licence					
a. No L plates	PL 10	No	2	£400	
b. No qualified supervisor	PL 20	No	2	£400	
c. Unqualified passenger	PL 30	No	2	£400	
d. Towing a trailer s.88 RTA 1972	PL 40	No	2	£400	
18. Driving with uncorrected defective sight, or	MS 70	No	2	£400	
Refusing to submit to an eyesight test s.91 RTA 1972	MS 80	No	2	£400	

189

Offence, Section and Act	D o E computer offence code	Compulsory disqualification (minimum 12 months except for special reasons)	Endorsement points	Maximum fine and/or imprisonment (offence committed on or after 1 May 1984) Magistrates' Court	Indictment	Remarks
19. Driving whilst disqualified						Triable either way.
a. by order of court	BA 10	No	6	£2000 and/ or 6 months	Fine and/or 12 months	
b. by being under age s.99(6) RTA 1972	BA 20	No	2	£2000 and/ or 6 months	Fine and/or 12 months	
20. No third party insurance s.143 RTA 1972	IN 10	No	4—8	£1000		
21. Contravention of traffic regs. on special roads other than by unlawfully stopping or allowing vehicle to remain at rest on part of special road on which vehicles are in certain circumstances permitted to remain at rest s.17(4) RTA 1984	MW 10	No	3	£1000		Motorway offences (see also 29)

No.	Offence	Code		Points	Fine
22.	Pedestrian crossing offences:				
	a. with moving vehicle	PC 20	No	3	£400
	b. with stationary vehicle s.25 RTRA 1984	PC 30	No	3	£400
23.	Failure to obey school crossing patrol s.28 RTRA 1984	TS 60	No	3	£400
24.	Contravening order prohibiting or restricting use of street playground by vehicles s.29(3) RTRA 1984	MS 30	No	2	£400
25.	Exceeding goods vehicle speed limit s.89 & Sch. 6 RTRA 1984	SP 10	No	3	£400
26.	Exceeding speed limit for type of vehicle s.89 & Sch.6 RTRA 1984	SP 20	No	3	£400
27.	Exceeding statutory speed limit on public road ss.81, 84, 89 RTRA 1984	SP 30	No	3	£400

Offence, Section and Act	D o E computer offence code	Compulsory disqualification (minimum 12 months except for special reasons)	Endorsement points	Maximum fine and/or imprisonment (offence committed on or after 1 May 1984)		Remarks
				Magistrates' Court	Indictment	
28. Exceeding passenger vehicle speed limit s.89 & Sch. 6 RTRA 1984	SP 40	No	3	£400		
29. Exceeding speed limit on special roads s.17(4) RTRA 1984	SP 50	No	3	£1000		Speeding on motorway
30. Theft or attempted theft of motor vehicle TA68, CAA81, Pt. III Sch. 4. RTA 1972	UT 20	No	8	£2000 and/ or 6 months	Fine and/ or 10 years	Triable either way. Covers S.1 TA 1968 and probably S.9 where property is a motor vehicle
31. Taking conveyance (or attempt) for own use or knowing it to be taken allows himself to be carried in or on it s.12/TA68, CAA81, Pt.III, Sch.4 RTA 1972	UT 40	No	8	£2000 and/ or 6 months	Fine and/ or 3 years	Triable either way. Not pedal cycles see S.12(5) TA 1968

32.	Having article for use in theft or taking of motor vehicle s.25/TA68 and Pt. III Sch. 4 RTA 1972	UT 30	No	8	£2000 and/ or 6 months	Fine and/ or 3 years	Triable either way. Where articles are to be used to steal from vehicles it is suggested offence does not attract endorsement/
33.	Manslaughter by driving Pt. II Sch. 4 RTA 1972	DD 60	Yes			Fine and/or Life imprison-ment	Triable only on indictment

DoE Sentence Codes

A	Imprisonment		N*	Cumulative Sentence
B	Detention in a place specified by the Secretary of State		P	Youth Custody Sentence
C	Suspended sentence of imprisonment		Q	Parent or Guardian Order
D	Suspended sentence supervision order		R	Borstal
E	Conditional Discharge		S	Compensation Order
F	Bound Over		T	Hospital/Guardianship Order
G	Probation		U*	Admonition
H	Supervision Order		V*	Young Offenders' Institution
J	Absolute Discharge		W	Care Order
K	Attendance Centre		X	Total period of partially suspended sentence of imprisonment
L	Detention Centre			
M	Community Service		*	Scottish Courts only.

Table 5: Fixed penalty offences

Relevant enactment	Description of offence	Endorsement
s.5(1) RTRA 1984	Using a vehicle in contravention of traffic regulation order outside Greater London	—
s.8(1) RTRA 1984	Breach of traffic regulation order in Greater London	—
s.11 RTRA 1984	Breach of experimental traffic order	—
s.13 RTRA 1984	Breach of experimental traffic scheme regulations in Greater London	—
s.16(1) RTRA 1984	Using a vehicle in contravention of temporary prohibition or restriction of traffic in case of execution of works etc	—
s.17(4) RTRA 1984	Wrongful use of special road	Obligatory, if committed as described in para. 4, Part III, Sch. 4, RTA 1972
s.18(3) RTRA 1984	Using a vehicle in contravention of provision for one-way traffic on trunk road	—
s.20(5) RTRA 1984	Driving a vehicle in contravention of order prohibiting or restricting driving vehicles on certain classes of road	—
s.25(5) RTRA 1984	Breach of pedestrian crossing regulations, except an offence in respect of a moving motor vehicle	Obligatory, if committed as described in para. 5, Part III, Sch. 4, RTA 1972
s.29(3) RTRA 1984	Using a vehicle in contravention of a street playground order outside Great London	Obligatory, if committed as described in para. 7, Part III, Sch. 4, RTA 1972

Relevant enactment	*Description of offence*	*Endorsement*
s.30(5) RTRA 1984	Using a vehicle in contravention of a street playground order in Greater London	Obligatory, if committed as described in para. 7, Part III, Sch. 4, RTA 1972
s.35(4) RTRA 1984	Breach of an order regulating the use etc of a parking place provided by a local authority, but only where the offence is committed in relation to a parking place provided on a road	—
s.47(1) RTRA 1984	Breach of a provision of parking place designation order and other offences committed in relation to a parking place designated by any such order, except any offence of failing to pay an excess charge within the meaning of s.46 RTRA 1984	—
s.53(5) RTRA 1984	Using a vehicle in contravention of any provision of a parking place designation order having effect by virtue of s.53(1)(a) RTRA 1984 (inclusion of certain traffic regulation provisions)	—
s.53(6) RTRA 1984	Breach of a provision of a parking place designation order having effect by virtue of s.53(1)(b) RTRA 1984 (use of any part of a road for parking without charge)	—
s.88(7) RTRA 1984	Driving a motor vehicle in contravention of an order imposing a minimum speed limit under s.88(1)(b)	—
s.89(1) RTRA 1984	Speeding offences under RTRA 1984 and other Acts	Obligatory
s.12(4) V(E)A 1971	Using or keeping a vehicle on a public road without licence being exhibited in the prescribed manner	—

Relevant enactment	Description of offence	Endorsement
s.22(1) V(E)A 1971	Driving or keeping a vehicle without required registration mark or hackney carriage sign	—
s.22(2) V(E)A 1971	Driving or keeping a vehicle with registration mark or hackney carriage sign obscured etc	—
s.16 RTA 1972	Unlawful carrying of passengers on motor cycles	Obligatory
s.22 RTA 1972	Failure to comply with traffic directions or signs	Obligatory if committed as described in the entry to Col. 5, Part 1, Sch. 4, RTA 1972 relating to this offence
s.24 RTA 1972	Leaving vehicle in dangerous position	Obligatory if committed as described in the entry to Col. 6, Part I, Sch. 4, RTA 1972 relating to this offence
s.32(3) RTA 1972	Breach of regulations relating to protective headgear for motor cycle drivers and passengers	—
s.33A(3) RTA 1972	Breach of regulations requiring wearing of seat belts	—
s.33B(2) RTA 1972	Breach of restriction on carrying children in the front of vehicles ·	—
s.36 RTA 1972	Driving motor vehicle elsewhere than on a road	—
s.36A(1) RTA 1972	Parking a heavy commercial vehicle on verge or footway	—
s.36B(1) RTA 1972	Parking a vehicle other than a heavy commercial vehicle on verge or footway	—

Relevant enactment	Description of offence	Endorsement
s.40(5)(a) RTA 1972	Breach of construction and use regulations	Obligatory if committed as described in the entry to Col. 5, Part 1, Sch. 4, RTA 1972 relating to an offence under s.40(5) but subject to the exception there mentioned
s.40(5)(b) RTA 1972	Using on a road a motor vehicle or trailer which does not comply with construction and use regulations	Obligatory if committed as described in the entry to Col. 5, Part I, Sch. 4, RTA 1972 relating to an offence under s.40(5) but subject to the exception there mentioned
s.81(1) RTA 1972	Contravention of any provisions of ss.68-79 RTA 1972 or Regulations under any of those provisions (requirements with respect to lights, reflectors etc)	—
s.84(1) RTA 1972	Driving vehicle without requisite licence	Obligatory if committed as described in the entry to Col. 5, Part I, Sch. 4, RTA 1972 relating to this offence
s.88(6) RTA 1972	Breach of provisional licence conditions	Obligatory
s.159 RTA 1972	Failure to stop vehicle on being so required by constable in uniform	—
s.15 GLC(GP)A 1974	Parking a vehicle on footways, verges etc	—
s.137 HA 1980	Obstructing a highway, but only where the offence is committed in respect of a vehicle	—

Appendix 4

Legal aid in criminal proceedings

Reproduced below is the letter of 27 March 1981 circulated by the Lord Chancellor's Department to Clerks of the Justices (see page 106). The Circular is Crown copyright and is reproduced with the permission of the Controller of Her Majesty's Stationery Office. Note that the figures are now out of date.

Dear Sir

Legal Aid in Criminal Proceedings

The Lord Chancellor has been taking stock of legal aid in criminal cases since he assumed Ministerial responsibility for it in July. He has not reached any conclusions as to the nature of any changes that may be required. Meanwhile he wishes to stress that his prime concern is that the administration of criminal legal aid should be such as to enhance the quality of justice.

The Legal Aid Act 1974 imposes the duty on courts considering applications for legal aid to exercise their discretion. The Lord Chancellor is firmly of the view that the indiscriminate grant or refusal of legal aid is a breach of this duty. He therefore asks that you should give the most careful consideration to the arrangements for determining applications for legal aid. Decisions on the grant of legal aid should be taken on the basis of an adequate knowledge of the facts and the arrangements must be such that the courts are properly acquainted with the precise nature of the charges and the grounds of the application, if necessary by calling upon the prosecution for information (*R* v *Highgate Justices ex parte Lewis* [1977] Crim LR 611). In this connection the application form devised by the Justices' Clerks' Society and The Law Society [see page 134] is commended.

If the criteria for the grant of legal aid (Para 2 H.O. circular 237/1972 and resumé of circulars—Annex B) are to be properly applied, the grounds for the application must be spelt out.

Applicants are entitled to have doubts arising on their applications resolved in their favour, but they are not entitled to the benefit of those doubts on the strength of vague applications. For example a simple statement that the applicant is in danger of losing his liberty or livelihood or, as the case may be, that the charge raises a point of law does not suffice. The application must set out the reasons why the applicant is in 'real jeopardy' of losing liberty or livelihood, or why the charge raises 'a substantial question of law'. In some cases where it is suggested that an applicant's previous convictions place him in 'real jeopardy' of losing his liberty, it may be necessary to disclose their nature. Where this is done and the application has been seen by a member of the Bench, steps must be taken to ensure that he does not hear the proceedings.

Some applications for legal aid are premature in the sense that the information required to determine them is not yet available. In some cases it may be desirable to postpone a decision until the applicant has had the benefit of advice under the green form scheme. Details of the scheme are set out in Annex C. It may transpire that the circumstances are such that what is really required is advice and assistance under the green form scheme rather than legal representation under section 28 of the Legal Aid Act 1974.

There are many claims on the funds available for legal aid and the Lord Chancellor is concerned that legal aid in criminal proceedings should secure value for money. This does not mean that courts should refuse legal aid where it is justified. It does mean that where legal aid is granted, every effort must be made to avoid waste. In particular it is essential to do everything possible to reduce waiting time to a minimum. Annex D contains an analysis of the cost of legal aid in the magistrates' courts showing that waiting time accounts for about 20% of a legal aid bill and on that basis costs something in the order of £8 million a year. In this connection the Lord Chancellor endorses the suggestions with regard to listing in Annex E.

Unnecessary attendances on formal remands can lead to substantial waste. This arises not only from the cost of the hearing. There is the cost of any waiting and travelling time as well. The Law Society has been invited to remind solicitors of the need to use to best advantage the funds available for legal aid. Accordingly, attendance by a solicitor acting under a criminal legal aid order is not necessary at a formal hearing unless he has an application to make or oppose, or the court appearance represents a convenient and economical opportunity for the solicitor to obtain any further instructions from his client that may reasonably be required. The Lord Chancellor has been informed by The Law Society that Area Committees will not sanction payment out of the Legal Aid Fund for attendances on remand which are not necessary on the basis of these criteria.

Unnecessary duplication of work also gives rise to waste. It does not further the interests of justice, does not benefit defendants and does not represent value for money. Steps must therefore be taken to avoid it. In particular applications for separate representation or change of solicitor should be carefully probed; it is not sufficient that the defendant is the client of a particular solicitor. Where the matter is not clear it is open to courts to ask the prosecution whether a defendant is charged with others. In addition the solicitor originally assigned to a case where separate representation is subsequently requested, should be asked to deal with questions of conflict in the first instance (*R* v *Solihull Justices ex parte Johnson* (1971) 140 JPN 198). It may well be that where a conflict does exist the assigned solicitor will be unable to act for any of the defendants.

The courts must inevitably rely heavily on what solicitors tell them about legal aid applications and legally aided cases. The profession has indicated that it will continue to co-operate with the Lord Chancellor in securing the effective administration of criminal legal aid. Where a solicitor appears to a court to be wanting in the standard of co-operation demanded by the profession, consideration should be given to raising the matter with that solicitor, and in the absence of a satisfactory explanation, reporting the matter to the taxing authority, i.e. the appropriate Area Committee of The Law Society. In this connection courts might wish to bear in mind the principles set out in the Lord Chief Justice's Practice Direction of 1977 to the Crown Court about allowance and disallowance of fees and expenses in legal aid cases, which is reproduced at Annex F.

The Lord Chancellor also asks courts to bear in mind that legally aided defendants should be asked to contribute to the extent that their means will allow towards the cost of their defence. He suggests that realistic down payments should be required in all suitable cases and that arrangements should be made to ensure that the question of a contribution order is considered in these cases to avoid the down payment becoming returnable by default. To assist them to make contributions which reflect the actual cost of representation courts might find it useful to ask the solicitor in the case to provide an estimate of his costs.

Finally the Lord Chancellor is very much in favour of the closest liaison between Justices' Clerks, The Law Society's Legal Aid Area Secretaries and local Law Societies. The proper administration of criminal legal aid depends on it.

Yours faithfully
J. G. H. Gasson

[*Annex A is the form of application for legal aid, updated and reproduced here at page 134*]

Annex B: Summary of principal Home Office circulars relating to Legal Aid in Criminal Proceedings

147/1968: Summary of the Provisions of the Criminal Justice Act 1967 relating to legal aid in criminal proceedings and of certain Regulations made under that Act.

149/1968: Fees and Expenses Regulations 1968.

231/1968: Amendment and amplification of 147/1968.

299/1970: Amendments to the General Regulations.

237/1972: Guidance about certain aspects of the legal aid scheme including the commendation to the courts of the Widgery Criteria as set out below.

The main factors which may point to eligibility for legal aid are [*as set out on page 105*]

61/1974: Introduction to Legal Aid Act 1974.

206/1974: Information leaflets about legal aid.

93/1976: Amendment of General Regulations relating to the power to order two counsel and advice on joint representation.

95/1977: Amendment of Regulation 7(6) of the Fees and Expenses Regulations.

170/1977: Abolition of the two-counsel rule.

97/1978: Guidance about the administration of the legal aid scheme including suggestions about listing which are reiterated in Annex E of this circular.

5/1979: Amendments to the Assessment of Resources Regulations.

60/1979: Amendment to the Fees and Expenses Regulations to provide inter alia for the payment of counsel in solicitor only cases.

43/1980: Legal Advice and Assistance Regulations 1980.

59/1980: Transfer of Functions Order transferring criminal legal aid and costs to the Lord Chancellor, and amendment of the General Regulations.

Annex C: The Legal Advice and Assistance (Green Form) Scheme

1. The Scheme is governed by Part I of the Legal Aid Act 1974, as

amended by the Legal Aid Act 1979, and the following regulations. The Legal Advice and Assistance Financial Conditions (Nos. 2, 3 and 4) Regulations 1979 (S.I.s 350, 1395, 1164) the Legal Advice and Assistance (Prospective Cost) Regulations 1980 (S.I. 1119) and the Legal Advice and Assistance Regulations (No. 2) 1980 (S.I. 1898).

2. Any person whose disposable income does not exceed £85 a week and whose disposable capital does not exceed £600 may apply to a solicitor for advice and assistance under the Scheme.

3. Advice may be given by the solicitor or, if necessary, by counsel on the application of *English law* to any particular circumstances which have arisen in relation to the person seeking advice and as to *any steps* that the person might appropriately take having regard to the application of English law. Assistance may be given in taking any steps on behalf of the person assisted or in assisting him to take them on his own behalf.

4. The cost of the advice and assistance available is limited to £40 unless approval for an extension is obtained from the appropriate committee of The Law Society.

5. The assistance may include representation before a court or tribunal, but only for those proceedings prescribed by regulation and with the approval of the appropriate committee of The Law Society. The prescribed proceedings are set out in schedule 4 of the Legal Advice and Assistance (No. 2) Regulations 1980. Criminal proceedings are not among those prescribed but the provision, formerly in section 2(4) of the Legal Aid Act 1974 and repealed by the Legal Aid Act 1979, by which representation under the scheme for proceedings in magistrates' courts or county courts could be authorised at the instance of or with the approval of the court has been preserved in regulation 19 of the same regulations. The cost of such representation is limited to £40.

6. A person wishing to obtain advice and assistance must apply to a solicitor who will complete the approved form (the Green Form). Before giving any advice and assistance the solicitor must assess the person's means in accordance with the relevant provisions of the Legal Advice and Assistance (No. 2) Regulations and determine any contribution in accordance with the scale prescribed in the same regulations. The solicitor is responsible for collecting the contribution and is reimbursed for the cost incurred over and above the contribution and within the prescribed limit by The Law Society from the Legal Aid Fund.

7. Legal advice and assistance is not available to any person in connection with any proceedings at a time when a civil aid certificate or criminal legal aid order is in force for the purpose of those proceedings.

Annex D: Criminal Legal Aid in Magistrates' Courts

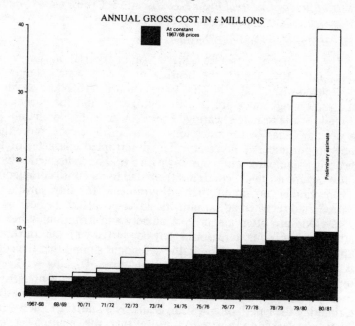

ANNUAL GROSS COST IN £ MILLIONS

At constant 1967/68 prices

*ANALYSIS OF SOLICITORS' BILLS IN STRAIGHTFORWARD CASES INVOLVING ONE
DEFENDANT ONLY

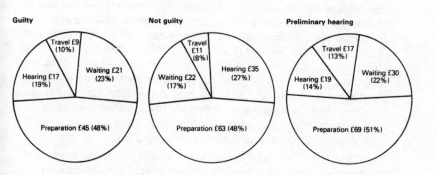

Guilty

Travel £9 (10%)
Hearing £17 (19%)
Waiting £21 (23%)
Preparation £45 (48%)

Not guilty

Travel £11 (8%)
Hearing £35 (27%)
Waiting £22 (17%)
Preparation £63 (48%)

Preliminary hearing

Travel £17 (13%)
Hearing £19 (14%)
Waiting £30 (22%)
Preparation £69 (51%)

£90 (excluding VAT)   £131 (excluding VAT)   £135 (excluding VAT)

* From a sample of bills paid in the first half of 1980

Annex E: Report of the Interdepartmental Committee on the distribution of Criminal Business between the Crown Court and the Magistrates' Courts Paragraphs 258—259.

The arrangement of court business

258. A number of witnesses criticised summary trial on the ground that, not infrequently, the hearing of a case which cannot be completed within half a day has to be adjourned to a date on which the same magistrates are free to sit together and the parties can attend for the resumed hearing. The adjournment is commonly for a week and may be for much longer, and in some cases more than one adjournment is necessary. This interrupted character of the hearing is compared unfavourably with a trial on indictment which, once begun, normally continues from day to day until completion. There can be no doubt that adjournments for any substantial period, and repeated adjournments, adversely affect the hearing of a case and are often a source of anxiety and irritation. When an adjournment is due to reasons solely connected with the court, it is apt to create the impression in the defendant's mind that the court is not interested in his case. The difficulties of listing work in a magistrates' court are well recognised: often the plea is not known in advance and, in cases known in advance to be contested, estimating the length of a hearing is largely a matter of guesswork. Justices' clerks do much to ensure that the man-power and accommodation available for the trial of cases are used to the greatest advantage. But justices' clerks have to rely upon advance information provided by the prosecution and the defence about the likely course and length of the hearing. We have not investigated to what extent interrupted hearings are avoidable and to what extent this cause for criticism can be removed, as this is not within our terms of reference. But we feel bound to refer to this feature as one which attracts criticism of summary trial, and grounds of criticism of summary trial inevitably lead to preference for trial on indictment irrespective of the gravity of the offence. Any improvement that can be achieved in the disposal of summary trials without the need for long or repeated adjournments during the hearing will, we believe, assist the proper distribution of criminal business.

259. One area where it seems to us that there is scope for streamlining procedures is in the arrangements for setting down a case for hearing for the first time. It is frustrating for a defendant to appear in court in answer to a summons and, perhaps having waited most of the morning, to find that, although he is ready to proceed, the case is automatically adjourned because he is pleading not guilty. We understand that many courts operate a system whereby defendants are notified when they receive the summons that only

guilty pleas (in practice the majority) will be heard on the return date. Not guilty pleas are automatically adjourned to enable the prosecution to prepare its case and arrange for the witnesses to be called. This saves a good deal of time for the court, the prosecution and witnesses by ensuring that a case is not prepared for a contest when the defendant intends to plead guilty. It also has the advantage of reducing the defendant's liability to costs in the event of his being ordered to pay them, since otherwise he may be required to pay the expenses of witnesses who have attended unnecessarily. The procedure admittedly has the disadvantage that a person pleading not guilty has to wait longer than a person pleading guilty for his case to be disposed of, but this is almost inevitable under any system because of the longer time it takes for both sides to prepare for a contested case. The advantage to the defendant of knowing that, unless he himself wishes to apply for an adjournment, he will usually have to make only one appearance in court is considerable, and we recommend that all courts not operating such a procedure should consider adopting it.

Annex F: Practice Direction: Allowance and disallowance by the Taxing Authority of fees and expenses under Legal Aid in criminal cases in the Crown Court ([1977] 1 All ER 542; [1977] 1 WLR 182)

1. It is the duty of the Taxing Authority to allow within the limitations imposed by the Legal Aid in Criminal Proceedings (Fees and Expenses) Regulations 1968 such fees and expenses as appear to him to be fair remuneration for work actually and reasonably done.

2. Where it appears to a Judge of the Crown Court being a High Court Judge, Circuit Judge or Recorder sitting in proceedings for which legal aid has been granted, that work may have been unreasonably done, e.g. if the legally assisted person's case may have been conducted unreasonably so as to incur unjustifiable expense, or costs may have been wasted by failure to conduct the proceedings with reasonable competence and expedition, he may make observations to that effect for the attention of the Taxing Authority. The Judge should specify, as precisely as possible, the item, or items which the Taxing Authority should consider or investigate on taxation. The precise terms of the observations should be entered in the Crown Court record.

3. It is not the function of the Judge to disallow or order the disallowance of fees and expenses. It is for the Taxing Authority to decide whether any disallowance should affect any individual counsel or solicitor and his decision will depend upon the circumstances.

4. Where the Judge has in mind that observations under paragraph 2 might be made he should inform the solicitor or counsel whose fees or expenses might be affected of the precise terms thereof and of his right to make representations to the Taxing Authority and give him a reasonable opportunity to show cause why the observations should not be recorded. This should normally be done in chambers at such time as the Judge in his discretion thinks proper. If the Judge then decides that the observations should be made he may announce this decision in open Court if of the opinion that it is in the interests of justice to do so.

5. If the Judge has made any such observations the Taxing Authority must afford an opportunity to the solicitor or counsel whose fees or expenses might be affected to make representations in relation to them.

6. Whether or not such observations have been made by the Judge the Taxing Authority may consult him on any matter touching the allowance or disallowance of fees and expenses, but if the observations then made by the Judge are to the effect mentioned in paragraph 2, the Taxing Authority should afford an opportunity to the solicitor or counsel concerned to make representations in relation thereto.

7. On taxation the Taxing Authority should have regard to all relevant information available to him from the Crown Court record, the documents in the case, or otherwise; the Judge's observations; any representations by the solicitor or counsel concerned in relation to them.

8. This practice direction does not apply to orders for costs under the Costs in Criminal Cases Act 1973, to taxation of costs in civil proceedings, nor to the exercise of the Court's inherent jurisdiction to order a solicitor to pay the costs thrown away.

Widgery CJ

Index